WINNING CHESS TACTICS

Learn the Secrets of Tactical Chess Today!

ABOUT THE AUTHOR

Bill Robertie is the world's best backgammon player and the only two-time winner of the Monte Carlo World Championships. Robertie is the author of seven backgammon books and the co-publisher of *Inside Backgammon*, the leading backgammon magazine. He also is a chess master, winner of the U.S. Speed Chess Championship, and the author of six chess books. Robertie's club and tournament winnings have allowed him to travel the world in style. He currently makes his home in Arlington, Massachusetts.

BACKGAMMON AND CHESS BOOKS
BY BILL ROBERTIE

501 Essential Backgammon Problems
Backgammon for Winners
Backgammon for Serious Players
Advanced Backgammon Volume 1: Positional Play
Advanced Backgammon Volume 2: Technical Play
Lee Genud vs. Joe Dwek
Reno 1986
Beginning Chess Play
Winning Chess Tactics
Winning Chess Openings
Master Checkmate Strategy
Basic Endgame Strategy: Kings, Pawns, & Minor Pieces
Basic Endgame Strategy: Queens and Rooks

WINNING
CHESS
TACTICS

Learn the Secrets of Tactical Chess Today!

Bill Robertie

Cardoza Publishing

Cardoza Publishing is the foremost gaming publisher in the world with a library of more than 100 up-to-date and easy-to-read books and strategies. These authoritative works are written by the top experts in their fields and with more than 7,000,000 books in print, represent the best-selling and most popular gaming books anywhere.

SECOND EDITION

| First Printing | October 2002 |
| Second Printing | March 2004 |

Copyright ©1996, 2002 by Bill Robertie
- All Rights Reserved -

Library of Congress Catalog Card No: 2002105876
ISBN:1-58042-075-3

Visit our new web site (www.cardozapub.com) or write us for a full list of Cardoza books, advanced and computer strategies.

CARDOZA PUBLISHING
P.O. Box 1500 Cooper Station, New York, NY 10276
Phone (800)577-WINS
email: cardozapub@aol.com
www.cardozapub.com

TABLE OF CONTENTS

1

INTRODUCTION

Winning at chess requires mastering two ways of thinking; **strategy**, creating the broad pattern of attack–laying out the overall plan for the deployment of your forces; and **tactics**, the details of hand-to-hand combat in chess–the thrusts and parries that determine whether pawns and pieces are won or lost.

FIRST WORD

By the time you've finished this book, you'll be able to start using these ideas in your own games. The results will be dramatic. You'll win more often and against stronger players, and your play will start to show some of the power and imagination that you've seen in the games of the masters.

Now let's get started!

Although both parts of the game are important, it's tactical chess that matters most. It doesn't matter how elaborate a winning plan you concoct if you lose a piece in the middle of it. If you're going to be a winner, the quickest way is to master the tactics of the game.

In this book we're going to show you the secrets of tactical chess. Instead of making clumsy threats, you'll learn how to use your pieces in coordinated attacks, shattering your opponent's position with a few deft strokes. Your pieces will multiply their power as you home in on the weak spots in your opponent's game. You'll see the power of pins, single and double forks, double attacks, skewers, discovered checks, double checks and attacks, attacking overworked pieces, and other powerful concepts including multiple threat tactics.

Now let's get started!

CHESS NOTATION

Chess notation starts by putting a coordinate grid over the chessboard.

The horizontal rows, or **ranks**, are numbered from 1 to 8. White's first row, the rank containing the White pieces, is number 1. The rank with Black's pieces is now number 8.

FIRST WORD

Chess notation is a simplified way of recording the moves in a chess game. By learning chess notation, you'll be able to follow the games and explanations in this or any other chess book. It's really quite easy.

Here's how it works.

The vertical rows, or **files**, are lettered **"a"** through **"h"**, with "a" starting on White's left and "h" on White's right.

Take a look at the diagram on the next page.

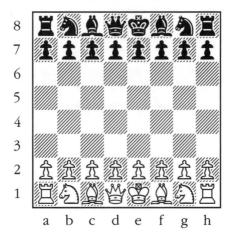

The notation system

THE NOTATION SYSTEM

This grid system lets us refer to any square on the board by a unique name. White's King is currently sitting on the square "e1." Black's Queen is on square "d8," and so on. In addition to the grid system, we have abbreviations for each of the pieces. Here they are:

ABBREVIATIONS FOR THE PIECES

King	K
Queen	Q
Rook	R
Bishop	B
Knight	N
Pawn	-

To indicate a move, we write down the piece that moved, and the starting and ending squares of the move. However, if a pawn is moving, we don't write anything more than the starting and ending squares. We use a dash to separate the starting and ending squares, and an "x" if the move was a capture.

SPECIAL NOTATIONS

Certain moves in chess have their own special notation.

• Castling King-side is denoted by "0-0." Castling Queen-side is denoted by "0-0-0."

• When promoting a pawn, indicate the promoted piece in parentheses: for instance, "a7-a8 (Q)" says that White moved a pawn to the a8 square and promoted it to a Queen.

• Capturing *en passant* is indicated by "ep" after the move: for instance, "d5xc6 ep" shows a pawn capturing *en passant* on the c6 square.

We use exclamation points and question marks to comment on the ingenuity or effectiveness of moves. Here's what they mean:

ANNOTATION COMMENTS
! means a good move.
!! means a brilliant, completely unexpected move.
? means an error.
?? means a gross blunder, probably losing the game.

3

THE POWER OF TACTICAL CHESS

When I teach chess to players of various strength, one question comes up, in different forms, over and over again. It goes something like this: "There's this one player, and he always seems to beat me! I don't know how he does it, but no matter how carefully I play, he always seems to find a way to win my pieces, one after another. What's his secret?"

FIRST WORD

Tactics is what chess is really all about. The players who have learned tactical chess are winners. Those who haven't, are losers. In this book, I'll show you the secrets of tactical chess. You'll learn what separates the winning players from the average Joes.

Armed with this knowledge, you'll win, and keep on winning.

Without even meeting this opponent, I can usually answer the question. "Your opponent knows the secret of *tactical chess*. He knows the basic winning patterns that recur in game after game, in the openings, middle games, and the endgames. Because he knows what to look for, he's always one step ahead of you. Until you master the secrets of tactics, he'll keep on beating you.

The basic idea of tactical chess is a simple one: Make moves that contain multiple threats, not just single threats. It's easy to respond to one threat. It's difficult (often impossible) to respond to two threats at once.

Learning tactical chess is learning how to pack multiple threats into single moves. Once you learn the techniques, you'll be like a boxer who can deliver combination punches instead of single lumbering shots, or like a basketball player who can fake the jumper and drive to the basket. Your moves will be more powerful, more forceful, more threatening. Opponents will be forced on the defensive from the beginning, and you'll be calling the shots.

Let's take a look at the difference between simple, linear chess, and powerful, tactical chess.

Take a look at this position:

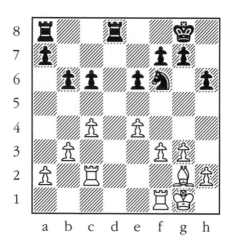

Diagram 2: White to move.

White and Black are even in material. It's White's move, and he sees a chance to make a threat. He plays **e4-e5**.

The pawn attacks the Black Knight on f6. That's a real threat, since a Knight is worth more than a pawn. If Black plays aimlessly, for instance moving h6-h5, White will play e5xf6 next turn, winning a Knight for a pawn. As we know, that would give White a considerable advantage.

But suppose Black notices the threat. What can he do?

Actually, defending against this particular threat is pretty easy. Black can simply move his Knight to any square where it's not under attack. He could go to d7, or e8, or h7, or h5. On any of these squares, the Knight would be at least temporarily safe from the White pieces. (The Knight wouldn't go to e4 or g4–it would be taken by the pawn on f3.)

Why was this threat so easy to defend against? Because it was just a *single threat*. White had only one idea–to capture the Knight on f6. All Black had to do was move the Knight, and he was safe. *Single threats are easy to guard against.*

Up until now, your chess games have probably consisted of a series of single threats. You attack one of your opponent's pieces; he moves it away. Then he attacks one of yours; you pull it back. Once in a while, you make a threat that he doesn't see, or he does the same to you. When that happens, one of you captures a piece for free. The player who does that most often goes on to win the game.

That's fine for beating beginners, but it won't work against more experienced players. They'll see your simple threats, and they'll always seem to have more of their own. To beat them, you'll have to start playing **tactical chess**.

Take a look at the next position:

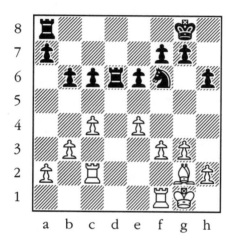

Diagram 3: White to move.

This position is similar to the last position, but there's a crucial difference. Now look what happens when White plays his threat, **e4-e5**. The pawn attacks the Knight on f6, as before. But now the pawn also attacks the Rook on d6! *One move, two threats.*

As before, Black can move his Knight to safety. But if he does that, he will lose the Rook on d6. Or, he can move the Rook, but then he will lose the Knight. He can guard against either threat individually, but not both at the same time. Since a Rook is more valuable than a Knight, he will undoubtedly choose to safety the Rook, and lose the Knight. But either way, he has a losing game.

White's move, e4-e5, is an example of a tactical idea called the **fork** or the **double attack**, two terms for the same thing. We'll see lots more examples of this idea in Chapter 10.

MULTIPLE THREATS

The above example illustrates the underlying idea behind all tactical play: *Use your pieces to create multiple threats at once.* When you learn to do that, it's as if you were able to make two moves at the same time–it gives you a tremendous advantage, one that your opponents won't be able to withstand.

Here's another example:

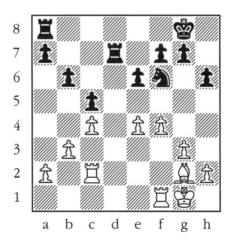

Diagram 4: White to move.

;ain, a similar position to our two previous examples.
gain, White moves **e4-e5** attacking the Black Knight.
And again, Black can save the Knight by moving it away.

But take a look at something else. By moving from e4-e5,
the White pawn has gotten out of the way of the Bishop
on g2. That Bishop now strikes all the way down the
board. In particular, it now attacks the Black Rook on a8!

White has used one move to launch two threats. This
time, only one threat comes from the pawn itself. The
other threat comes from the Bishop, whose attack on the
Rook was uncovered by the move of the pawn. This is an
example of **discovered attack**, and we'll see more
examples in Chapter 9.

Black can't respond to both threats at the same time. If he
moves the Rook, he loses the Knight. He has one try–he
can move the Knight so as to block the Bishop's attack on
the Rook, with the move **Nf6-d5**. But then White wins
the Knight anyway with **c4xd5**.

The essence of chess tactics is this simple idea: Learn to
use your pieces to execute multiple threats with single
moves. In the following chapters of this book, we'll show
you the recurring patterns of tactics: the pin, the Knight
fork, the skewer, and so on.

By the time you've mastered the basic tactical pattersn,
you'll be amazed at how quickly your results will im-
prove. Players that used to beat you with ease will now
be throwing up their hands in surrender. It won't take
magic–just tactics!

THE PIN

Suppose your opponent has a less valuable piece and a more valuable piece on the same line– a rank, a file, or a diagonal. You attack the less valuable piece. If your opponent moves the less valuable piece to safety, the more

FIRST WORD
The most basic tactical idea is called the **pin**. The idea of the pin is simple. Let's have a look...

valuable piece behind it will come under attack and be lost. Rather than surrender the more valuable piece, your opponent will choose to abandon the less valuable piece.

PRESSURE AND ADVANTAGE
Let's look at a simple example.

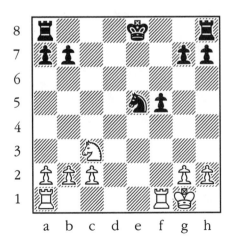

Diagram 5: White to play.

In Diagram 1, the material is even. Each side has two Rooks, a Knight, and five pawns. White has an opportunity to win a pawn outright, by playing Rf1xf5. Black would then retreat his attacked Knight, and White would be a pawn ahead. That's an inviting line of play, and many players would choose it without hesitation.

But White can do better! Here's a wonderful guiding principle, which will serve you very well in your chess career: *When you see a good move, don't make it immediately. Look for a better one first.*

Before grabbing the pawn, White looks around the board. He notices that Black's Knight and his King are arranged on the same file. (In Book 1 of this series, "Beginning Chess Play," we learned that the vertical rows of squares are called **files**, while the horizontal rows of squares are called **ranks**.) Moreover, the Knight is undefended. The right way to exploit the situation is with a pinning move, so White plays **Rf1-e1!**

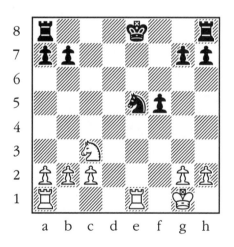

Diagram 6: Black to play.

The Rook attacks the Knight, but the Knight can't legally move. If Black moves the Knight, he would expose his own King to check, which is against the rules. Black can't defend the Knight, so he is helpless to prevent its loss. Next turn White will play **Re1xe5,** and he will be a Knight ahead.

Sometimes the pin is only the first step to winning material. Take a look at Diagram 7 below.

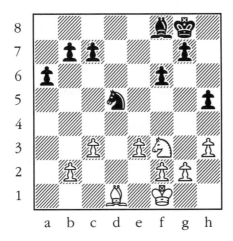

Diagram 7: White to play.

As before, White sees the opportunity for a pin, and plays **Bd1-b3!** The Bishop attacks the Black Knight, which can't move because it must guard the Black King from attack by the White Bishop. Unlike the last problem, however, Black has a defensive resource; alertly, he plays **c7-c6.**

Take a look at the next diagram.

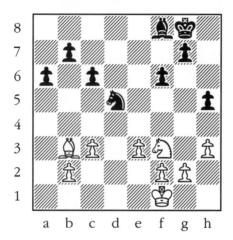

Diagram 8: White to play.

The Knight is still pinned, but it's now solidly guarded by the pawn on c6. If White captures the Knight with Bb3xd5 check, Black recaptures with c6xd5. That's an even trade, a Bishop for a Knight. Can White do better?

Indeed he can. The key is to remember that a piece pinned against its own King can't move, so just bring up the reserves.

White piles on the pressure with **e3-e4!**

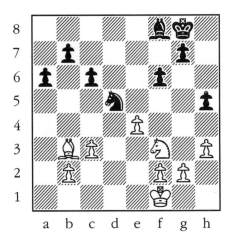

Diagram 9: Black to move.

Now White threatens to capture the Knight with a lowly pawn, and against this threat there is no defense. Next turn White will play **e4xd5,** winning a Knight for a pawn.

Incidentally, White could easily have gone astray in the position of Diagram 9.

Suppose, instead of playing e3-e4, he had attacked the Knight another way, with c3-c4.

Take a look at Diagram 10 on the next page.

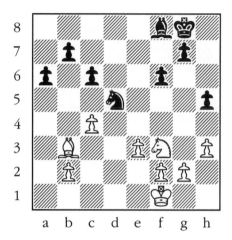

Diagram 10: Black to move.

The pawn attacks the Knight, but at the same time it blocks the action of the Bishop! Now Black can save himself by alertly playing Nd5-b4. (He could also have moved it to e7 or c7.) Since the pawn blocks the Bishop's line, the Black King is not now in check.

DEFENDING AGAINST THE PIN
Does the pin always win?

No, not always. Sometimes the defender can thwart the pin, but he must be alert. Don't assume that a piece is lost just because your opponent has pinned it. Look around for possibilities of your own.

We'll take a look at two examples of successful defenses against a pinning threat.

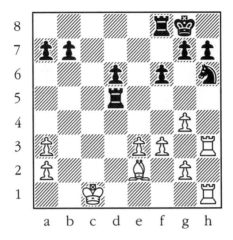

Diagram 11: White to move.

White sees an opportunity for a winning pin, and without checking too closely, plays **Be2-c4?**

The Bishop pins the Black Rook against the Black King, which looks to be a crusher, since Black can't defend the Rook.

What can he do? Rather than give up, Black looks for a counter-shot, and finds one.

Do you see it?

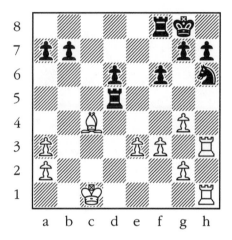

Diagram 12: Black to move.

Black executes a pin of his own, and plays **Rf8-c8!**

Now the Black Rook pins the White Bishop to his King. The Bishop can't move, and this time there's no defense. Black will capture the Bishop next turn and be a piece ahead.

The diagram on the next page shows a different method of defense.

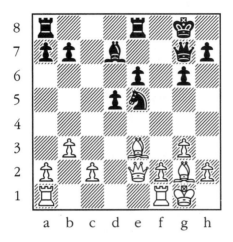

Diagram 13: White to move.

White notices Black's Knight and Queen lined up on the long black diagonal, and sees a chance to win the Knight. He pins it against the Queen with the powerful-looking **Be3-d4.**

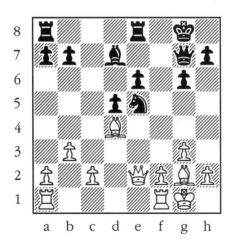

Diagram 14: Black to move.

The Bishop attacks the Knight, and by moving, allows the White Queen to participate in the attack as well. (That's an example of **discovered attack**, which we'll cover more fully in a later chapter.) White reasons that if Black moves the Knight, White will take Black's Queen with his Bishop. Otherwise, White will just snap off the Knight next turn.

But Black spots a hole in White's play and saves himself with an unexpected shot: he plays **Ne5-f3 check!**

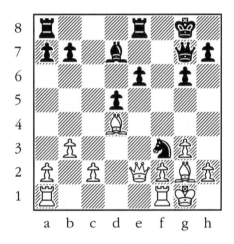

Diagram 15: White to move.

Because the Knight is giving check, White doesn't have time to take Black's Queen. Getting out of check is always top priority. White can get out of check quite easily, of course–he just takes the Black Knight with either his Queen or his Bishop. But no matter which piece he uses, Black next turn will play **Qg7xd4,** capturing the White Bishop. It's an even trade, and Black will be out of danger.

Here Black took advantage of the fact that *only pins against the enemy King are absolute.* By absolute, I mean that the pinned piece can't legally move. A pin against some other piece, like the Queen, isn't absolute–the pinned piece can legally move, but probably won't. However, if the pinned piece can move with a greater threat, like a check, the pin can be broken.

MORE PINS

Now let's take a look at some more examples of pinning. In the problems that follow, try to work out the best line of play by yourself first. (It might help to set the positions up on your own board, to get the flavor of playing an actual game.) Then read below the diagram to see the solution. The first problems are the easiest; the later problems are a little more difficult.

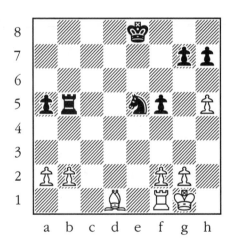

Diagram 16: White to move.

White is a pawn ahead in Diagram 16, which might be enough to lead to a long, slow win in the endgame.

However, White would like to find a quicker way to win.

One possibility is to pin the Black Knight against the King by playing Rf1-e1. The Knight won't then be able to move, although it's defended by the Black Rook, so White wouldn't immediately capture it. The pin would have set up a powerful threat, however, moving the pawn next turn from f2 to f4, picking off the pinned Knight.

It's a good idea, but Black would have an easy defense. In response to Rf1-e1, Black would just play Ke8-f7. By moving the King he would unpin the Knight. Then if White tried f2-f4, Black would just move the Knight away.

Does White have something even stronger?

Yes he does. Notice that the Black Knight isn't the only piece lined up with the Black King. The Black Rook is also on a line with the King, in this case the diagonal from a1 to e8. White can exploit this with a different, and deadlier, pin: **Bd1-a4!**

Now the Bishop attacks the Black Rook, which, unlike the Knight, is completely undefended. Nothing can stop the Bishop from capturing the Rook next turn. White will then be a Rook ahead, with an easy win.

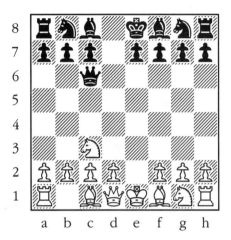

Diagram 17: White to move.

In *Beginning Chess Play* we learned that it's not a good idea to develop the Queen too early. A Queen roaming around the board in the early stages of the game is subject to all sorts of attacks and traps.

In Diagram 17, Black has violated this rule and brought his Queen out before any of his other pieces have been mobilized. Still, the Queen looks pretty safe, not too far from Black's camp and well away from any White pieces.

But White can explode this illusion of safety with a quick, deadly pin! Notice that Black's Queen and King are on the same diagonal. White spots this flaw in Black's position and sees a nasty way to exploit it–he plays **Bf1-b5!**

The Bishop pins the Black Queen to the Black King

behind it. Black can capture the Bishop with **Qc6xb5,** but then the guarding Knight snaps off the Queen: **Nc3xb5.** White has won a Queen for just a Bishop. Black is doomed.

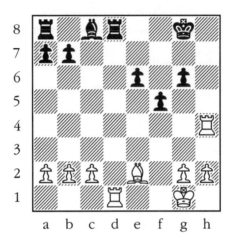

Diagram 18: Black to move.

Not all pins are artfully created. Sometimes your opponent will walk right into one if given the chance.

In Diagram 18, the game is about even. Black could simply exchange Rooks by playing Rd8xd1 check, and White would reply Be2xd1. Then Black could develop his remaining pieces with moves like Bc8-d7 and Ra8-c8, with a good game.

Instead of following that simple plan, Black inverts the order of moves, and runs into disaster. In Diagram 18, he brings his Bishop out first, with **Bc8-d7??** White sees his opportunity and plays **Rh4-d4!**

Out of nowhere, a pin has materialized on the d-file. If Black moves his Bishop, White's Rook will capture the Black Rook behind it. If Black leaves his Bishop where it is, White will pick it off next turn since Black can't bring any other pieces to defend. A moment's inattention led Black into a lost game.

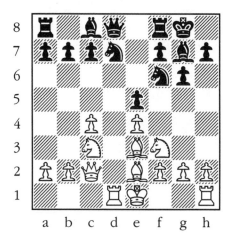

Diagram 19: White to play

Sometimes a player can be deceived by an apparently compact and solid position. In Diagram 19, Black has just castled on the King-side, thinking that his position was quite secure.

White alertly spotted the flaw in Black's game. White's Rook on d1 is pinning the Black Knight on d7 against the Black Queen. Black can't move the Knight without losing his Queen for a Rook. Since the Knight is pinned, its defense of the Black pawn on e5 is an illusion.

White quickly takes advantage before Black can rearrange his pieces for a better defense. He plays **Nf3xe5!**, winning a pawn.

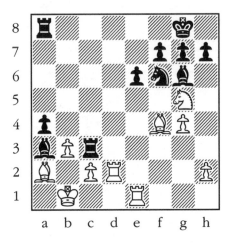

Diagram 20: Black to play.

The pin in Diagram 20 is a little more difficult to spot. A great habit to develop is the following: *Look at all your pieces and trace out, in your mind's eye, their lines of movement.*

This is an especially useful exercise during the dead time when your opponent is thinking about his move. It will reinforce in your mind the possibilities open to you, and let you spot combinations more easily.

In Diagram 20, Black starts with a capture: **a4xb3.** White naturally recaptures with **Ba2xb3.** So far so good. White still appears to have a solid position. But now Black springs the trap: **Rc3xb3 check!** White wants to recapture the Rook, but he can't! His pawn on c2 is pinned by

the Black Bishop all the way back on g6. He has to mo
his King, **Kb1-a2,** after which Black retreats his Rook to
b7 with an easily won game.

It's easy to miss a play like this by not noticing the action
of the Bishop along the entire diagonal from g6 to b1.
Trace out the actions of your pieces in your mind before
moving, and you'll see traps like this one more fre-
quently.

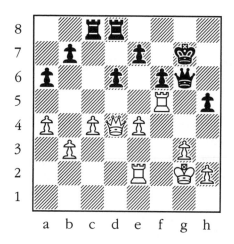

Diagram 21: White to play.

Sometimes the deadliest traps are prepared by a defensive move. Your opponent gets lulled into a false sense
of security from the feeling that you're merely respond-
ing to his threats. This makes him careless, and he
overlooks the real point of your move.

In Diagram 21, Black has just played his pawn from **h7-
h5.** This move contains a small threat of pushing the
pawn forward to h4 (relying on the fact that the pawn on

g3 would be **pinned** and unable to capture) and then exchanging it for the White pawn on g3. This line of play would open up White's King position a little bit. It's not really a dangerous threat, but White sees that he can prevent it with a move that contains a subtle but deadly counterthreat.

He plays **h2-h4.**

Normally Black might see the threat contained in this move. But, convinced that White was simply defending, Black blindly continues with his own plans: He plays **e7-e6,** trying to evict the White Rook from its dominating post.

Now White springs his trap; he plays **Rf5-g5!** The Black pawn on f6 can't capture the Rook, because it's pinned by the White Queen. If Black plays **Qg6xg5,** White just replies **h4xg5,** pocketing a Queen for a Rook.

Black didn't notice that White's pawn move had a double purpose–both stopping the advance of Black's pawn, and simultaneously guarding the g5 square so White could play his Rook there next turn.

Be alert, and look for any hidden threats behind your opponent's moves.

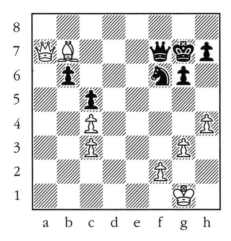

Diagram 22: Black to play.

Sometimes just one pin won't do the trick. In Diagram 22, Black surprises his opponent with not one but two maneuvers based on a powerful pin.

Black begins with the dangerous **Nf6-e4!** The Knight is unguarded but White can't capture because his Bishop is pinned to his Queen by the Black Queen. Meanwhile, Black threatens to swoop down and capture the White pawn on f2 with his Queen backed up by his Knight. His idea is Qf7xf2 check, Kg1-h1, and then Ne4xg3 checkmate!

Since White can't take the Knight, he has to look for another means of defense. He could protect the pawn on f2 by playing Qa7-a2, but that would leave the Bishop defenseless. Black would just play Qf7xb7 and be a piece ahead.

Instead White finds his only defense; he plays **f2-f3.** Black can't capture the pawn on f3 with his Queen. (Do you see why?)

But Black doesn't need to fall into that trap. Instead he moves his Knight again: **Ne4-d6!** The Knight now attacks the Bishop, which is still pinned to the White Queen.

White is helpless against this new attack. The best he can do is capture a pawn with **Qa7xb6.** Black then plays **Nd6xb7,** winning a piece and incidentally guarding the pawn on c5. With an extra piece, Black should win without much trouble.

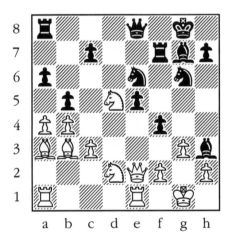

Diagram 23: Black to play.

Sometimes a pin can be created with a threat or a trap. In Diagram 23, Black plays **f4-f3!,** hoping to eventually organize an attack on the White King's position. Still, at first glance, the move looks like an oversight. White is attacking the pawn twice, with his Knight and his Queen, and Black is only defending it with one piece, his Rook. "Ah" says White, "Looks like my poor opponent just gave me a free pawn. Thank you very much." White plays **Nd2xf3.** He sees that if Black plays Rf7xf3, he can respond with Qe2xf3. So far so good.

But Black has other ideas. After Nd2xf3, Black plays **Bh3-g4!** pinning the Knight to the Queen. White is helpless, as none of his other pieces can come to the defense of the Knight. Next turn Black will play Bg4xf3 or Rf7xf3, remaining a piece ahead.

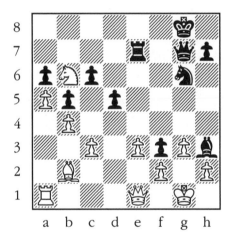

Diagram 24: Black to move.

Sometimes a pin is meant not to win material, but as a stepping stone to a further threat.

In Diagram 24 Black has a brilliant mating attack in mind. He begins the attack with a move based on two powerful pins; he plays the shocking **Ng6-f4!!**

The Knight steps boldly into a nest of pawns. But what can White do? The pawn on the g-file is pinned by the Black Queen. And the pawn on the e-file is pinned against the Queen by the Black Rook at e7. The g-pawn *can't* capture, while the e-pawn can, but only at the cost of the White Queen.

White plays **Qe1-d2,** unpinning the e-pawn and now threatening to capture the impudent Knight. But Black doesn't wait around for that. He plays **Nf4-e2 check!** White's King has only one safe square; he plays **Kg1-h1.** But then Black replies with **Bh3-g2 checkmate!** Cut off from the rest of its army, the White King was trapped in its own fortress of pawns.

GAINING A TEMPO

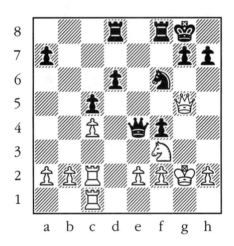

Diagram 25: Black to move.

In Diagram 25 Black has managed to pin White's Knight on f3 against his King. Still, how does Black take advantage of this? The Knight seems securely protected by both the White King and the White pawn on e2. Besides, the White Queen is in the area to provide more protection if necessary, and the other Black pieces don't seem poised to attack. How can Black make progress?

Black starts with the innocuous-looking move **h7-h6.** The pawn attacks the White Queen, which will of course simply move away. On second thought, though, that's not so simple after all. The Queen has a severe shortage of squares! The Black Knight effectively controls d5, g4, and h5. In fact, the only safe square for the Queen is h4. So White plays **Qg5-h4.**

Now Black strikes at the Queen again with **g7-g5!** Once again the Queen is caught short of moves. The only choices now are to retreat the Queen to h3 or capture the pawn on h6.

"A pawn's a pawn" says White, and he snaps off the Black pawn with **Qh4xh6.**

Now Black reveals the point of his play; he advances again with **g5-g4!** The pawn has advanced from g7 to g4 in two turns, and now the pinned White Knight is lost. The maneuver from g7 to g5 is known as **gaining a tempo.** By attacking the Queen, Black forces it to move and thus gains time to advance on to g4 before White can organize a defense.

THE PIN SET-UP

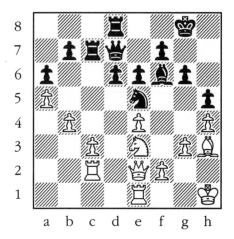

Diagram 26: Black on move.

White's last move, **Bg2-h3,** set up a pin and created a threat. Black, focussing only on his own plans, didn't see the pin or the threat. Instead he played **Rd8-c8,** trying to capture the White pawn on c3.

White then sprung his trap with **Ne3-d5!** The Black pawn on e6 is pinned against the Black Queen by the White Bishop, so Black can't capture the Knight. Meanwhile, Black's undefended Bishop is under attack by the Knight, and so is his Rook on c7. (This is our first example of a **knight fork**, the subject of the next chapter. Here the fork is made possible by a **pin**.)

Black has a choice of saving the Bishop and losing a Rook for a Knight, or saving the Rook and losing a whole Bishop. Since a Bishop is worth more than the difference between a Rook and a Knight, he chooses to safety the

Bishop with **Bf6-d8.** White then chops off the Rook, **Nd5xc7,** and Black recaptures, **Qd7xc7.** The material advantage of a Rook for a Knight should win for White in the endgame.

Black have avoided this disaster by paying careful attention to his opponent's moves.

Ask yourself: *"Does my opponent's last move contain a threat? Does it attack a piece? Does it pin something? What's my opponent thinking about?"*

You're not the only player at the board with ideas. The fellow across the table may have a few of his own. Try to figure out what he's planning, and you'll avoid walking into *his* traps.

MULTIPLE PINS

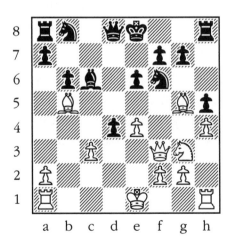

Diagram 27: White on move.

Our last problem in this chapter shows that pins don't have to occur singly; they can come in groups, and be overpowering.

In Diagram 27 Black has just played **Bb7-c6,** blocking a check from the White Bishop at b5 on the Black King. He expects White to exchange Bishops, after which he will recapture with his Knight, with a secure position.

But White has no such intention. Instead he crosses Black up (literally) with the brilliant **e4-e5!!,** a move involving no less than three pins!

Take a look. The Bishop on c6 is pinned against the Black King by the Bishop on b5 (so it can't capture the White Queen). It's also pinned against the Black Rook by the White Queen. (The pinning of a single piece in two different directions is known as a **cross-pin**.) In addition, the Black Knight on f6 is pinned against the Black Queen by the Bishop on g5, and the Knight is now attacked by the White pawn on e5.

With all these pins in operation, Black couldn't survive very long. He tried **Bc6xb5,** and White replied **e5xf6.** This threatened f6xg7, which would have been crushing, so Black blocked that threat with **g7-g6.**

Finally White played **Qf3xa8,** picking up a full Rook. Black resigned.

5

KNIGHT FORKS

The Knight fork is the second most common tactical idea in chess, next to the pin. A Knight fork simply means that a Knight moves and attacks two enemy pieces at the same time. Of course, any piece has the power to fork two enemy pieces under the right circumstances.

FIRST WORD

What makes a Knight fork such a powerful maneuver is the Knight's odd way of moving. When a Knight attacks the King, Queen, Rook, Bishop, or pawn, it cannot itself be under attack in return! Only an enemy Knight is immune to the power of a Knight fork.

What makes a Knight fork such a powerful maneuver is the Knight's odd way of moving. When a Knight attacks the King, Queen, Rook, Bishop, or pawn, it cannot itself be under attack in return! Only an enemy Knight is immune to the power of a Knight fork.

SUCCESSFUL KNIGHT FORKS

Let's look at a couple of examples of winning Knight forks.

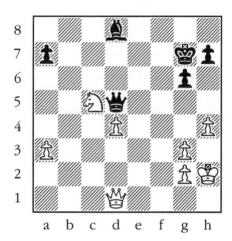

Diagram 28: White to move.

In Diagram 28 White has two extra pawns, but he's finding it difficult to make progress. Black's Queen is powerfully situated in the center of the board, controlling key squares and blocking the progress of White's d-pawn.

White, however, sees an clever idea for pushing forward. He plays **Qd1-f3!** The White Queen attacks the Black Queen in the center of the board. Black doesn't want to exchange Queens, since that would both undouble White's pawns and reduce the game to an ending where White's two extra pawns would be enough to win the game.

But Black's not worried, because White's last move looks like a blunder to him. Doesn't it leave the White pawn on d4 unguarded? Without hesitating too long, Black snaps off the loose pawn: **Qd5xd4.**

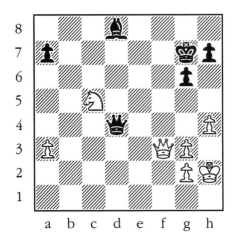

Diagram 29: White to move.

Now White springs his trap: **Nc5-e6 check!** The Knight attacks Black's King, Queen, and Bishop, in one brilliant stroke. Black has no way to capture the rampaging Knight. He will have to move his King to h6, and then White will pick off the Queen with Ne6xd4. A devastating shot.

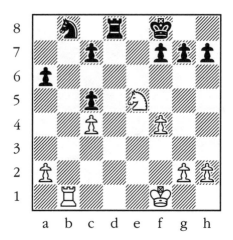

Diagram 30: White to move.

In Diagram 30, White trails Black by a pawn in the material count, but his pieces are more actively placed. Although no Knight fork seems to be available, White can create one with a startling move. Do you see it?

White plays **Rb1xb8!,** capturing the Black Knight. Black isn't concerned at first, since the Knight was securely protected. He recaptures with **Rd8xb8.**

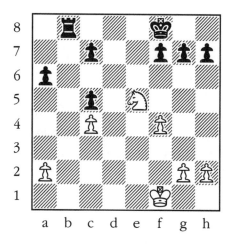

Diagram 31: White to move.

Now White is ready to execute a Knight fork. He plays
Ne5-d7 check, attacking the King and the Rook simultaneously. Black has no choice; he must save his King
with **Kf8-e7.** Finally White plays **Nd7xb8.** He has won
a Rook and Knight at the cost of only a Rook, leaving him
a Knight ahead with a routine win in store.

Notice two key elements of White's combination. First,
no fork was possible in Diagram 30, so White *substituted
one Black piece for another.* By replacing the Black
Knight with the Black Rook, White removed the guard-
ian of the d7 square and made a Knight fork possible.

Second, and most important, was this: *White found his
combination by examining the captures and checks in the
position.* This is a crucial element behind successful
tactical play. Checks and captures are *forcing* moves.

They cut down on your opponent's possible replies, since he must recapture a piece (in response to a capture) or move his King (in response to a check). If you know what your opponent's about to do, it's much easier to visualize the position a move or two down the road.

Get in the habit of looking at all the forcing moves available. As you do, you'll begin to see more and more winning possibilities like the earlier combination in Diagram 30.

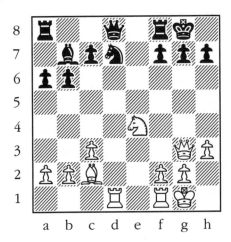

Diagram 32: White on move.

By combining Knight forks with pins, a whole variety of powerhouse attacking ideas open up. Take a look at Diagram 32.

White and Black are even in material in Diagram 32, and at first glance Black's game seems solid enough. But White reduces his opponent to rubble with a couple of sledgehammer blows, based on a pin and a Knight fork.

White starts with the forcing **capture Rd1xd7!** Black must recapture or be a piece down, so he plays **Qd8xd7.**

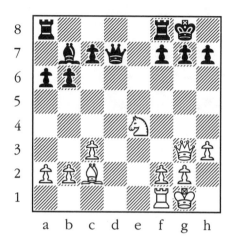

Diagram 33: White to move.

Now White lowers the boom with **Ne4-f6 check.** (A *forcing* check.) The Knight forks the Black King and the Black Queen. Can Black capture the Knight? No! His pawn on g7 is pinned against the Black King by the White Queen on g3. Black has to move **Kg8-h8,** and White plays **Nf6xd7,** winning.

DEFENDING AGAINST THE KNIGHT FORK

A Knight fork isn't always a winning maneuver. In some cases, a clever player can turn an apparently winning fork back on his opponent.

Let's look at an example:

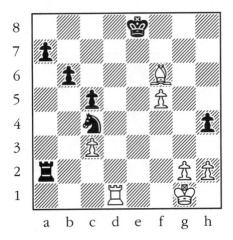

Diagram 34: Black to move.

Material is even in Diagram 34. Each side has a Rook, four pawns, and a minor piece. (Knights and Bishops are sometimes called **minor pieces**, to distinguish them from the Queens and Rooks, which are known as **major pieces**. Knights and Bishops are approximately equal in value.)

But Black sees a chance to win a pawn based upon a clever Knight fork. Unfortunately for him, White has seen the possibility too, and knows that he has an ingenious defense. Let's watch how play proceeds.

Black begins with the startling **Ra2xg2 check.** White naturally plays **Kg1xg2.** Now Black plays **Nc4-e3 check.** The Knight forks the White King and the White Rook. White doesn't panic, but quietly plays **Kg2-f3.** f3 is a very important square for the White King, as we shall see. Black concludes his combination by playing **Ne3xd1.**

He has given up a Rook, and won back a Rook and a pawn. So far so good. But now White pulls out a real surprise, which he had foreseen before Black began his combination; he plays **c3-c4!** Take a look.

Diagram 35: Black to move.

White's last little pawn move is not so innocuous after all! Take a look at the Black Knight. Where can it move to? The White King guards the squares e3 and f2, and will capture the Black Knight if it moves there. The White Bishop on f6 now guards the squares b2 and c3 (as a result of moving the c-pawn) and will capture the Knight if it tries to escape that way. The Knight has no safe squares at all! Next turn, White will play Kf3-e2, followed by Ke2xd1, capturing the Knight.

(Black can try to delay the process by harassing the White Bishop with Ke8-f7, but White will just retreat, Bf6-e5, after which Black won't be able to attack it any more.)

Remember this about Knights: They're most effective in the center of the board, where they have a full range of movement. They're weak on the edges and the corners of the board.

A Knight on a center square has eight other squares to move to. A Knight on the edge, as here, can only move to four squares–it's only half a Knight. Old-timers have a saying to warn of this limited mobility: "A Knight on the rim spells trim." Remember it.

MORE KNIGHT FORKS

Now let's look at some more examples of Knight forks.

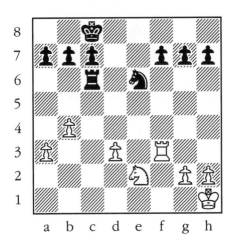

Diagram 36: Black to move.

Even a Knight is not necessarily immune from the power of a Knight fork. In Diagram 36, Black notices that White's collection of pieces do not cooperate well together. He finds the right way to exploit this–the Knight fork **Ne6-d4!**

The Knight attacks the White Rook and the White Knight. "What's the problem?" asks White. He captures the Knight with **Ne2xd4.** Now Black reveals the point of his play; he swoops down with **Rc6-c1 check!** Suddenly White is doomed. He can only play **Rf3-f1,** after which Black captures **Rc1xf1, checkmate.**

In Diagram 36, the White Knight had the job of guarding the c1 square. When the Knight moved to capture the Black Knight, the vital square was left undefended. Black was quick to capitalize.

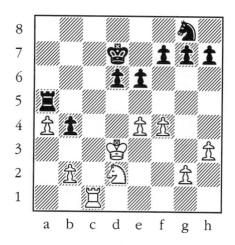

Diagram 37: White to move.

When you see that your opponent has left a piece or a pawn unguarded, *don't assume that he has just over-looked your threat!* Give your opponent credit for having a brain too, and take a quick check around the board. Ask yourself just what your opponent can do if you grab the unguarded material. A moment's pause could save you a game.

Diagram 37, White could defend his attacked pawn on
with a simple, solid move, b2-b3. Instead he plays
Nd2-c4!

Instead of asking himself, "Why didn't White make the
obvious defensive move? What's he planning?" Black
just assumes that White has made a mindless oversight.
Blindly, he grabs the pawn, **Ra5xa4.** He's quite pleased
with himself.

Not for long. White shows he had an idea after all. He
plays **Nc4-b6 check!** Oops. Black must move his King,
and White pockets the Rook: **Nb6xa4.**

Greed is good, but combine it with a little caution and
common sense.

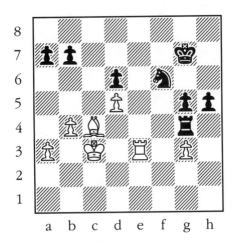

Diagram 38: Black to move.

White is a pawn down in Diagram 38, but he's hanging
on tenaciously. Black uses a Knight fork to smash

through White's resistance.

Black plays the startling **Rg4xg3!** White has no real choice, since Black is now threatening to capture White's Rook. He has to play **Re3xg3.**

Now Black's Knight settles things. He hops in with **Nf6-e4 check!** and White is finished. After White moves his King, Black will capture the undefended Rook. Not only has Black won a pawn, but his two passed pawns can now march down the board.

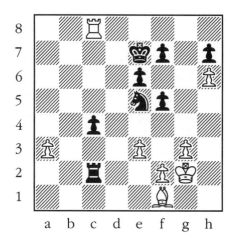

Diagram 39: Black to move.

Once you're in the habit of checking your opponent's moves for possible threats, you'll notice a real improvement in your results. But you can take this process one step further. *If you see one threat, look around for another one.* A good move can contain multiple threats, not just the most obvious one.

In Diagram 39, Black makes a strong move–**Ne5-g4!** The move contains *two* threats, not just one. Do you see them?

White sees the obvious threat, **Rc2xf2 check,** winning a pawn. Unfortunately, he can't prevent that threat. It's not crushing, however. In response, he'll be able to play Kg2-g1, containing his loss to only one pawn.

But hasn't Black left a pawn of his own unguarded? So White assumes. White plays **Rc8xc4,** picking off the Black pawn. He thinks Black will continue with Rc2xf2 check, and material will still be even.

But Black doesn't have to play that way! Moving the Knight to g4 had another, more hidden, threat. Now Black springs his trap. He plays **Ng4xe3 check!** The Rook on c2 is pinning the pawn on f2, so White can't recapture. He must move his King, and the Rook on c4 is lost to the Knight.

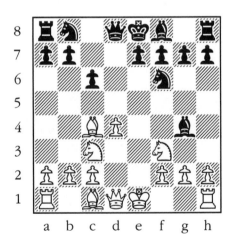

Diagram 40: White to play.

In Diagram 40, White can win a pawn and destroy the safety of Black's King's position with a neat combination based on a Knight fork.

White begins with **Bc4xf7 check!** Black has to reply **Ke8xf7.** White then plays **Nf3-e5 check!,** forking the King and the Bishop. Although the Knight was pinned by the Black Bishop, White doesn't have to be worried because he's moving the Knight with **check.** Black has nothing better than **Kf7-e8.**

Finally White plays **Ne5xg4.** Black recaptures with **Nf6xg4,** and White concludes with **Qd1xg4.** He has won a pawn, and Black's King has lost the right to castle.

Remember this idea, as it occurs in various forms in many different openings.

MULTIPLE KNIGHT FORKS

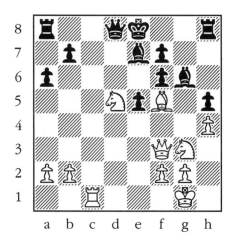

Diagram 41: White to play.

Black seems to have a solid defensive structure in Diagram 41. But White blasts his way to victory with a series of powerful blows, including two Knight forks.

White starts with the forcing capture **Bf5xg6.** Black must recapture, **f7xg6.** Next White makes the first of his Knight forks, **Nd5-c7 check,** forking the Black King and the Black Rook. The Knight is protected by the Rook on c1, so Black can't capture it with the Queen. Instead Black plays **Ke8-f7.**

Does White now capture the Rook in the corner? No! Instead he remembers this maxim: *When you see a strong move, look for a better one.* White looks and finds a better move, **Qf3-b3 check!**

Black's King can't go to e8 or g8, where it would still be in check. Instead he has a choice between f8 and g7. It doesn't really matter which square Black chooses. Black moves **Kf7-g7.**

White concludes his elegant combination with the crushing fork **Nc7-e6 check!** The Knight forks the Black King and the Black Queen. Black must move his King, losing the Queen. He's finished.

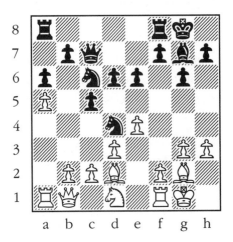

Diagram 42: Black to move.

In Diagram 42, Black sacrifices a pawn, then makes a seemingly innocuous move to get it back. His move sets a trap which White, in his haste to protect his extra pawn, simply overlooks. Black then uncorks a smashing series of Knight forks.

Black starts with a peculiar-looking move: **c5-c4!** The pawn is apparently completely unguarded. Has Black missed something? White doesn't see any problems, so he plays **d3xc4,** pocketing a pawn.

Black now plays **Nc6-e5!** "Hmm," says White, "Black's Knight is attacking my pawn on c4. Black's also attacking the pawn with his Queen. No problem, though, I'll just defend the pawn again." White plays **b2-b3,** supporting the pawn on c4.

Black's not going to play Ne5xc4. That would lose the

Knight for just a pawn. It looks like White is just a pawn ahead. Or is he?

Black strikes out in another direction. He plays **Ne5-f3 check!** White naturally captures with **Bg2xf3.** Now the other Knight hops in, **Nd4xf3 check!**

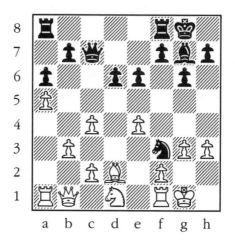

Diagram 43

Take a look. The Black Knight is forking the White King and the White Bishop. White plays **Kg1-g2.** Now Black takes the Bishop, **Nf3xd2,** forking the White Queen and the White Rook! After White saves his Queen, Black will take the Rook on f1 with his Knight, remaining a whole Rook ahead.

How could White have saved himself? When Black played Nc6-e5, White needed to notice that this move was not a simple threat against the pawn on c4 but was itself a fork. Black's Knight was forking the pawn on c4 and an empty square–f3! At this point White needed to let the pawn on c4 go and defend himself with a move like Bd2-c3, protecting the Bishop. Black would have regained his pawn, but White would still be in the game.

ANALYZING POTENTIAL KNIGHT FORKS

Not all Knight forks lead to a winning position. Like all ideas in chess, a potential Knight fork has to be carefully checked. Ask yourself these questions:

• **Have I anticipated all my opponent's replies?**

• **Is the sequence of moves I expect really forced?**

• **What would I do if I were in my opponent's shoes?**

Thinking like this can avoid some embarrassing surprises.

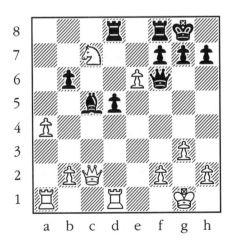

Diagram 44: White to move.

Take a look at Diagram 44. White sees the opportunity for a Knight fork winning Black's Bishop. Without checking carefully, he plays this combination.

He starts with **b2-b4,** attacking the Black Bishop. Black sees what is coming, but decides to play along since he also sees a refutation. He plays **Bc5xb4.** White now plays his fork with **Nc7xd5.**

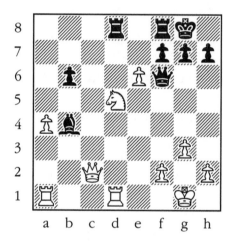

Diagram 45: Black to move.

The Knight now forks Black's Queen and Bishop. Black will have to save his Queen, but notice that all the squares where the Queen can move to guard the Bishop are attacked by the White pieces. The squares f4 and h4 are guarded by the pawn on g3, the Knight guards e7 and c3, and the White Rook guards d4. It looks like Black will have to settle for Qf6xe6, after which White can play Nd5xb4, finishing a Knight to the good. At least, that's what White expected before playing his combination.

But Black has seen further! Instead of moving his Queen, he floors White with an unexpected counterpunch: **Rd8xd5!** Instead of meekly moving his Queen, he rips off the White Knight.

Surprised by this turn of events, White recaptures with **Rd1xd5.** And now Black reveals his real point: **Qf6xa1 check!**

White had overlooked that his Rook on d1 had the double job of guarding the Knight on d5 and the other Rook on a1. (This is an example of the theme of the **overworked piece**. We'll see more examples in a later chapter.) Instead of finishing a Bishop ahead, White ends up a Knight behind.

THE SKEWER

The skewer is the inverse of the pin. In a pin, you attack a less valuable piece, which can't move because a more valuable piece lies behind it. In a **skewer**, you attack a

more valuable piece, which *must* move, exposing a less valuable piece to the rear.

SKEWER STRATEGY

Let's take a look at a couple of examples.

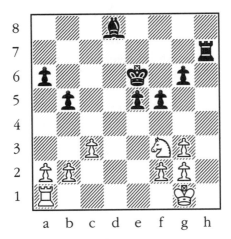

Diagram 46: Black to move.

Black plays **Ke6-d5?** He thinks he's being aggressive, moving his King to attack White's pawns on the Queenside. But White uses a skewer to expose Black's last move as a blunder. He plays **Ra1-d1 check!**

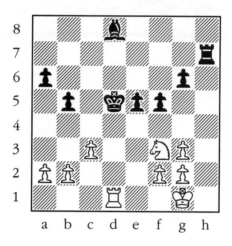

Diagram 47: Black to move.

Take a look. The Black King is attacked by the White Rook, so Black has no choice; he must move the King out of check. Let's say he moves **Kd5-c4.** But now the Black Bishop on d8 is helpless. White swoops down with **Rd1xd8.** He's used the skewer attack to win a Bishop.

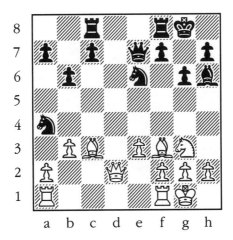

Diagram 48: Black to move.

White has just played b2-b3? He was hoping to drive away Black's annoying Knight at a4, thinking that Black might retreat the Knight to c5. Instead, Black plays **Na4xc3!**, capturing the White Bishop. "No problem," thinks White. "I have the Bishop well protected." He responds with **Qd2xc3.**

But now Black has created the opportunity for a skewer. He plays **Bh6-g7!** attacking the White Queen.

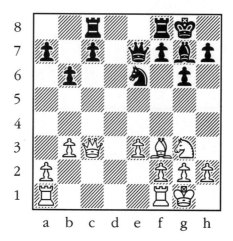

Diagram 49: White to move.

White's Queen isn't trapped, of course. He can move it to any number of squares. But no matter where he moves it, he will lose the Rook on a1 to Black's Bishop. Since a Rook is worth more than a Bishop, Black will be well on his way to victory.

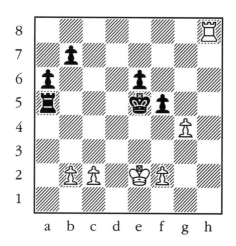

Diagram 50: Black to move.

White has just played g2-g4, attacking the Black pawn on f5. The Black pawn is securely protected, by the Black pawn on e6 and the King on e5, so Black does not need to fear losing material. But wait! Isn't the White pawn on g4 unprotected? Can't Black just snap it off and win a pawn?

That's what Black thought. He played **f5xg4??**, thinking he was winning a free pawn. Only when White whipped out **Rh8-h5 check!** did Black realize what was happening. Black had to move his King (it didn't matter where) and White continued with **Rh5xa5,** winning a Rook through a skewer attack.

Remember, your opponent is entitled to have ideas too. Try to figure out what he may have had in mind before you grab material.

Diagram 51: White to move.

71

In Diagram 51, the players have come down to the late stages of an endgame, with the result of the game still in doubt. While both sides have a minor piece, White has an extra pawn, and his King is better positioned to help the pawn advance to a Queen.

Many endgames of this type end in a draw. White wins if he can Queen his pawn, but that's not easy to do. All Black has to do to draw is to exchange his Knight for the pawn. Then White would have a King and Bishop against Black's lone King, and White wouldn't be able to effect a checkmate. (If you're not sure of this, set up the pieces on a board and try it yourself.)

White, however, sees a way to force a win in this position. He starts with a skewer, **Bc8-b7 check!** The Bishop checks the King and attacks the Knight behind the King. Black naturally moves his King to a square where it protects the Knight: **Ke4-f4.** White now exchanges pieces, **Bb7xf3,** and Black recaptures, **Kf4xf3.**

Diagram 51a

Now what? If White pushes his pawn, h3-h4, Black plays Kf3-g4 and captures the pawn next turn. The solution is to use the King to shepherd the pawn.

White plays instead **Kf6-g5!!** By keeping the Black King out of g4, White ensures that the pawn will be able to Queen. Next turn White will play h3-h4, then h4-h5, h6, and so on to h8. Black is doomed.

In this diagram the skewer didn't actually win any material; it just cleared the way for the White pawn to advance unimpeded.

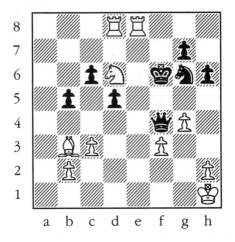

Diagram 52: White to move.

In Diagram 52, White notices Black's King and Queen lined up on the same file, raising the possibility of a skewer with Re8-f8. Unfortunately, Black's Knight on g6 guards the skewering square. White's solution? He moves there anyway!

White plays **Re8-f8 check.** Black captures the Rook with **Ng6xf8.** But now the other Rook swings into action: **Rd8xf8 check.** This time Black has no defense. He moves **Kf6-g5,** and White takes the Queen with **Rf8xf4.** Black can recapture the Rook, but White is left with two extra pieces and an easy win.

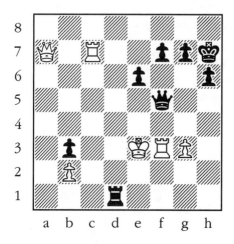

Diagram 53: Black to move.

Black trails by a whole Rook in Diagram 53, but White's pieces are somewhat out of play, far from their King. Black can use the exposed position of White's King to set up a skewer which pierces through White's defenses.

Black plays **Rd1-d3 check!** The Rook attacks the King and, behind the King, the White Rook. The Black Rook is guarded by the Black Queen, so White has little choice; he plays **Ke3-f2.** (Ke3-e2 would lose in a similar fashion.) Black then crashes through with **Qf5xf3 check.**

White has lost his key defensive Rook and now can't withstand the combined attack of the Black Queen and the Black Rook. White plays **Kf2-g1,** and Black sets up a nice finish with **Rd3-d1 check.** White's only escape square is **Kg1-h2,** and then Black delivers checkmate with **Qf3-h1 mate.** (Rd1-h1 was also mate.)

White's extra Rook was an illusion, since his pieces were so far from his King. In the crucial part of the board, Black had the preponderance of material all along.

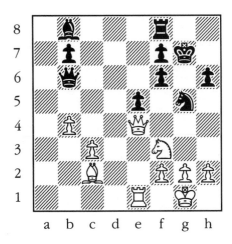

Diagram 54: White to move.

White can set up a winning skewer in Diagram 54, but it requires some preparation first.

With White's Queen and Bishop lined up on the diagonal b1-h7, White would like to be able to move into the h7 square. Right now that square is guarded by the Black Knight on g5. Incidentally, the Black Knight is also attacking the White Queen and the White Knight. Clearly, the key to Black's defense is that annoying Black Knight.

So take it off! White plays **Nf3xg5.** Black replies with **f6xg5,** to give his King some escape room. (If he played instead h6xg5, White would swoop down with Qe4-h7 checkmate.)

Now White plays **Qe4-h7 check.** Black moves his King to the newly-created escape square, **Kg7-f6.** Take a look.

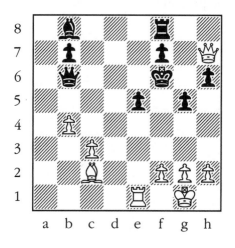

Diagram 54a

White's maneuvers have forced Black's King onto a line with the undefended Black Queen over on b6. Now White caps his imaginative play with **Qh7xh6 check!**

The White Queen skewers the Black King against his own Queen. After the King moves, White plays **Qh6xb6,** and the game is effectively over.

A DEFENSIVE SKEWER

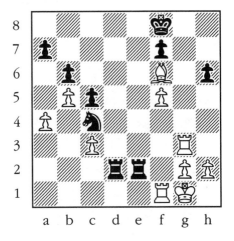

Diagram 55: Black to move.

In our earlier examples in this chapter, we looked at skewers that crushed our opponent and won decisive amounts of material. But a skewer can also be a defensive maneuver, useful in salvaging an otherwise lost position. Diagram 55 is a case in point. Black's two Rooks doubled on the second rank put terrible pressure on White's game. Seeing the possibility for a direct win, Black moves in for the final coup. He plays **Nc4-e3.**

The Knight attacks White's Rook on f1, and also combines with the two Black Rooks to attack the pawn on g2 a third time. Black expects White to move the Rook on f1 to safety, after which he will capture the pawn on g2, with a winning game.

But White sees the chance for a brilliant defensive maneuver, based on a skewer. He starts by playing the preliminary move **Bf6-g7 check,** forcing Black to move his King, **Kf8-e8.** Now White plays an unexpected shot, **Rg3xe3 check!,** sacrificing his Rook for Black's Knight. Black naturally replies **Re2xe3.** What's White up to?

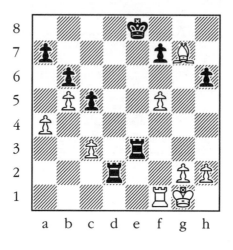

Diagram 55a

Finally White reveals his point: **Bg7xh6!** The Bishop skewers the two Black Rooks on the c1-h6 diagonal. White will capture one Rook with his Bishop, remaining two pawns ahead, with excellent winning chances in the endgame.

Notice that White's initial check with the Bishop had a dual point; to move the Black King to the e-file, so that White could capture the Black Knight *with check*, forcing Black to respond; and to move the Bishop so that it could reach the crucial diagonal from the square h6, since the g5 square was guarded by a Black pawn. It's often little finesses like this which make elaborate combinations possible.

DISCOVERED CHECK

You move a piece, and announce check. But the check isn't coming from the piece you moved in a discovered check, but from another piece located behind it on a file or diagonal.

FIRST WORD

The **discovered check** is a powerhouse winning idea which you won't want to overlook.

The idea is this:

If the piece you actually moved has created some threats, your opponent won't have time to deal with them–he has to get out of check first!

PRINCIPLES OF DISCOVERED CHECKS

Let's look at a couple of examples to get a better idea of this tactic.

See diagram 56.

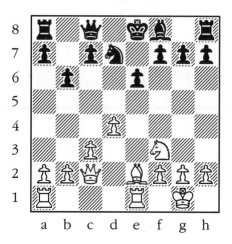

Diagram 56: White to move.

In Diagram 56, White plays **d4-d5!** apparently sacrificing a pawn. The pawn looks free to Black, so he grabs it with **e6xd5.** "A pawn's a pawn," says Black.

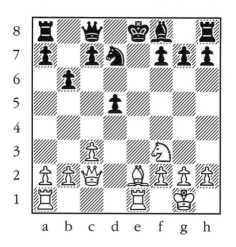

Diagram 56a: White to move.

"Not always," thinks White. He reveals the point of his play with **Be2-a6 discovered check!**

Take a look. The Bishop isn't the piece giving check. It's actually the White Rook at e1. The Rook's attack against the Black King was "discovered" when the White Bishop moved off the e-file.

Meanwhile the White Bishop becomes a rogue piece, free to make threats anywhere along its lines of attack. In this case, the Bishop is attacking the Black Queen at c8. Black would like to save the Queen and capture the pesky Bishop, but he can't. He must get out of check first. Black can play Bf8-e7, or Ke8-d8, but in either case his Queen is lost.

Now another example:

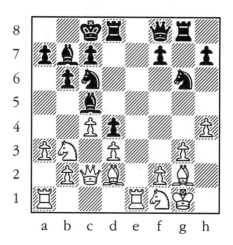

Diagram 57: Black to move.

In Diagram 57, White is a pawn ahead with what appears

to be a tight and well-secured position. White's Bishops control fine open diagonals, his Rook on e1 controls the e-file, and his Queen and Knights are developed, albeit modestly. Black's pieces do not appear especially threatening. There is certainly no sign of a discovered check in the air. Or is there?

Watch Black blast White's position open with a few sledgehammer blows. He starts with **Ng6xh4!,** an unexpected shot. White naturally recaptures, **g3xh4.** Suddenly Black has managed to pry open the g-file, leading directly to White's King.

The blows continue as Black plays **Rg8xg2 check!!** White has little choice now, he must recapture with **Kg1xg2.**

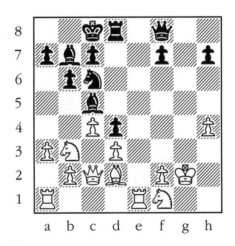

Diagram 57a: Black to move.

Look at how the position has changed in two moves. At the cost of a Rook, Black has managed to move White's

King to the h1-a8 diagonal, where all that stands between the King and Black's Bishop is the Black Knight at c6. Black now delivers the final coup, **Nc6-b4 discovered check!**

White is helpless. If he *weren't* in check, he could capture Black's arrogant Knight with the pawn on a3. But in the actual position, he *has* to get his King out of check first. No matter how he does it, Black's next move will be **Nb4xc2,** capturing the Queen and incidentally, forking the two White Rooks. White can regretfully resign.

MORE DISCOVERED CHECKS

Now that the pattern is clear, let's look at some more examples of discovered checks.

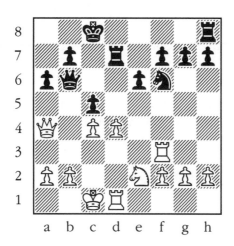

Diagram 58: White to move.

Material is even in Diagram 58, although White's pieces are more aggressively placed. Still, Black has no obvious weak spots, and it's not clear how White can make progress. Let's see how White conjures up a crushing discovered check from apparently unpromising beginnings.

White starts with an unexpected shot, **Rf3xf6!** "What's this all about?" says Black. "My Knight was solidly defended." He naturally recaptures with **g7xf6.**

Now White launches the next surprise in his combination, **Qa4xd7 check!!** Wow! First White sacrifices a Rook, and now his Queen. Again Black recaptures, **Kc8xd7.**

Now White reveals the point of his surprising play–**d4xc5 discovered check!** The pawn moves aside, revealing a check from the Rook back on d1. Meanwhile, the Black Queen is lost. After the Queen is captured, White will have a Rook and a Knight against Black's lone Rook, a winning advantage.

Now we can see why it was important for White to start his combination by capturing the Black Knight on f6. If he hadn't, Black could have answered Qa4xd7 with Nf6xd7, and no discovered check would have been possible. Brilliant play by White.

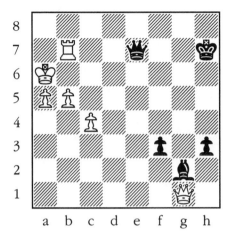

Diagram 59: Black to move.

White has just played Rb8-b7, pinning Black's Queen against his King, and apparently winning the game. But Black has a surprise in store for him, based on the power of the discovered check.

Black plays **Qe7xb7 check!** White has to reply **Ka6xb7.** And now Black reveals his point with **f3-f2 discovered check!**

The Black Bishop on g2 now checks the White King. Meanwhile, the Black pawn has advanced to f2, attacking the White Queen. The best White can do is **Qg1xg2,** but then Black plays **h3xh2.** Black will soon have two new Queens to replace the one he sacrificed. White gives up.

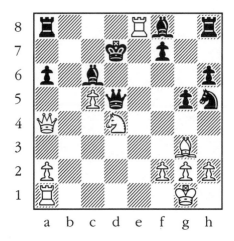

Diagram 60: White to move.

White is down a Bishop in Diagram 60, but his active pieces have Black under a lot of pressure. In particular, Black's King is under assault from all sides. Here's how White finishes the game.

White starts by ignoring his attacked Rook and playing instead **Nd4xc6!** Now Black has many choices, but some are clearly bad:

> • He can capture the Knight with Qd5xc6, but White then replies Ra1-d1 check, and Black's King will not be able to maintain its defense of the Black Queen. (Don't overlook the activity of the White Bishop on g3.)

> • He can capture the White Rook with Ra8xe8, but then White wins the Black Queen with Nc6-b4 discovered check!

With these grim possibilities facing him, Black tries a different capture; he plays **Kd7xe8.** Now if White plays Nc6-d4 discovered check, Black has a saving defense: Qd5-d7!

But instead, White has a different idea. He plays first **Ra1-e1 check.** Now the Black King can't move to e7 or d8 because of the White Knight, so he has to try **Ke8-d7.** But now White plays **Nc6-b4 discovered check,** and there's no way to save the Black Queen. An intricate and inspired combination.

8

DOUBLE CHECK STRATEGY

By putting the enemy King under attack from two pieces at the same time, you reduce his options considerably. He won't be able to capture *either* checking piece, since the other piece will still be giving check. And in the same way, blocking the line of attack of either piece will also be insufficient.

FIRST WORD

The **double check** is the most devastating of all chess tactics. As in the discovered check, a piece moves, giving check to the enemy King from another piece behind it on a file or diagonal.

But in this case, the moving piece itself gives check!

The only defense to a double check is to move the King. Nothing else will work. That's what gives the double check such awesome power.

USING THE DOUBLE CHECK
Let's look at an example of the double check.

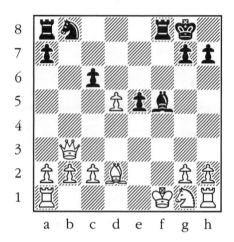

Diagram 61: Black to move.

Black is a Queen down in Diagram 61. Ordinarily, White would win easily. In fact, if it were White's turn, a simple consolidating move like Ng1-f3 or Kf1-e1 would secure White's position. But instead it's Black's move, and he has a crushing shot in mind.

Black plays **Bf5-d3 double check!**

Take a look. By moving, the Bishop exposes an attack on White's King from the Black Rook on f8. But in addition, the Bishop itself attacks the White King from d3.

What's White to do? He could take the Bishop easily enough, but still leaves him in check from the Black Rook. He could block the Rook's attack with Ng1-f3, but then he's still in check from the Bishop. No, he must move his King. But squares are limited. The e2 square is guarded by the Bishop, and the f2 square by the Rook.

That leaves White with just one legal move! He plays **Kf1-e1.** And finally Black swoops down with **Rf8-f1, checkmate!**

The power of the double check was that White's possible replies were so constrained. Only a King move would do, and the only one available walked right into checkmate.

Now let's look at a few more examples of this diabolical stratagem.

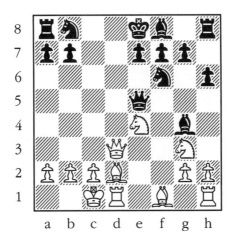

Diagram 62: White to move.

In Diagram 62, Black has moved his Bishop to g4, attacking White's Rook. A lesser player might meekly move the Rook to e1, or perhaps block the attack by moving Bishop to e2.

White hasn't the time for such defensive maneuvers. Instead he simply announces checkmate in three moves.

He begins with the electrifying **Qd3-d8 check!!**

Black is shocked, but he makes the only play: **Ke8xd8.**
Now White stuns him again with **Bd2-a5 double check!**
Quite unexpected.

What can Black do? He must move the King in response
to a double check. The squares c7 and d7 are off limits,
so his choice is between c8 and e8. No matter where he
moves, however, White's next blow is **Rd1-d8.** Extraor-
dinary play!

INVERTING THE ORDER OF MOVES

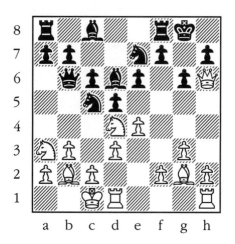

Diagram 63: White to move.

In Diagram 63, White would like to find some way for his
Queen to deliver checkmate on the g7 square. One
possibility is to play Nd4xe6, threatening Qh6-g7 checkmate. (The Queen would be backed up by the Bishop on
b2.) However, Black could refute this try by playing

Nc5xe6, guarding the g7 square with his Knight.

Another possibility is Nd4-f5, again threatening mate at g7. Again, however, Black would have a defense. This time he would play Ne7xf5, again guarding the g7 square with a Knight.

What's White to do? He finds an answer by *inverting the order of his moves*, which is often a tremendously useful tactic. Instead of moving the Knight to prepare to move the Queen to g7 next, what if he moves the Queen there first?

White sees a combination and plays first **Qh6-g7 check!!** Black is stunned, but he has no choice; he plays **Kg8xg7.**

Now White uncorks a double check, **Nd4-f5 check!** Black is in check from both the Knight on f5 and the Bishop on b2. He must move the King, but where? The Bishop attacks f6 and h8, and the Knight controls h6. Black must play back, **Kg7-g8.**

Then White administers the coup de grace, **Nf5-h6 checkmate!**

If not for the power of the double check, Black could have organized a defense, since he had many pieces in the critical area. The double check short-circuited Black's communications, forcing him to deal with the attack with just his lone King.

TWO DOUBLE CHECKS!

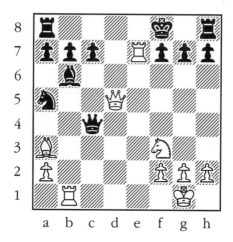

Diagram 64: White to move.

White trails by two pawns in Diagram 64, but obviously has the makings of a strong attack against Black's King. The best way to finish the game off, however, isn't immediately clear. White would like to play Qd5xf7 check, but Black could reply to that with Qc4xf7, breaking White's attack. Meanwhile White's Queen on d5 is unprotected, and Black is threatening Qc4xd5.

After a little thought, White finds the direct route to checkmate, based on two double checks, back to back! White plays **Re7xf7 double check!** The Black King is attacked by the White Rook and also the Bishop back on a3. If Black tries Kf8-e8, White swoops down with Qd5-d7 checkmate. Black tries to hide in the corner: **Kf8-g8.**

Now White finishes up with **Rf7-f8 double check** and **mate!** The Black King is now in check from the White

Queen and the White Rook. The Rook is guarded by the White Bishop on a3, so Black can't capture it with his King. Both White pieces are under attack, but Black can't capture them both at once. Game over.

UNDERMINING THE BASE

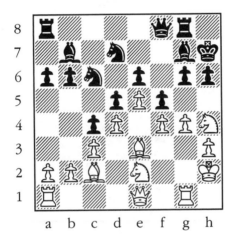

Diagram 65: White to move.

In Diagram 65, White uses a double check, not as a decisive blow to finish the game, but as a tactic to break through Black's fortress of pawns. In the starting position, Black's position looks cramped but defendable. White's pieces are all aimed at the f5 square, but Black has this point well-fortified. If White tries something direct, like g4xf5, g6xf5, Nh4xf5, e6xf5, Black is still holding on quite easily.

White's approach is worth remembering: Instead of blasting away at the head of Black's formation (f5), White undermines it by striking at the base (g6).

White starts his combination with **Nh4xg6!** Unwilling to surrender a key pawn, Black recaptures: **Kh7xg6.** Now White uncorks **g4xf5 double check!** By capturing on f5 with a double check (pawn on f5, Rook on g1), White cuts through all Black's defenses. Black replies **Kg6-f7.**

Now White continues with **f5xe6 check.** Black plays **Kf7xe6,** and White keeps coming with **f4-f5 check!** Take a look at the next diagram:

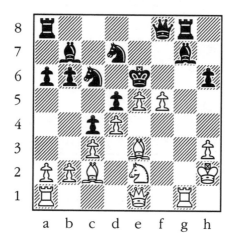

Diagram 65a

Although White only has two pawns for his lost Knight, the rest of his pieces have sprung to life behind his pawn avalanche.

Black plays **Ke6-e7** (moving to f7 allows White to play e5-e6 check), and White plays **Qe1-h4 check!** Black plays **Ke7-e8,** and White follows up with **f5-f6.** With Bc2-g6 check looming, Black throws in the towel.

DISCOVERED ATTACK

A discovered attack is similar to a discovered check. But whereas in a discovered check, the object of attack was always the enemy King, in a **discovered attack** the target can be any piece.

FIRST WORD
Strong tactical play makes for exciting games, especially when you can spring a discovered attack on a hapless opponent.

Take a look at Diagram 66.

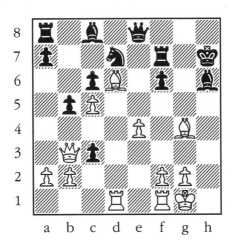

Diagram 66: Black to move.

POWER CHESS–
THE DISCOVERED ATTACK!

Black has an extra piece in Diagram 66, but he's under a lot of pressure. His King-side pawn position has been torn open, and White's Bishops sweep the board. White is even threatening Bg4-h5, pinning the Black Rook to the Black King. If Black could simplify the position by trading some pieces, he'd have excellent chances to win in the endgame.

But how does he get there?

Black sees an opportunity to eliminate some pressure by using a discovered attack. He plays **Nd7xc5!** The Knight takes a pawn and attacks the White Queen. At the same time, the Knight *discovers* an attack on the unguarded White Bishop at g4 from the Black Bishop at c8.

White's faced with two threats–what can he do? With his Queen under attack, he has nothing better than **Bd6xc5.** Black then plays **Bc8xg4,** and he's solved his problems while winning another pawn in the process.

Diagram 67 on the next page shows another, more brutal, example.

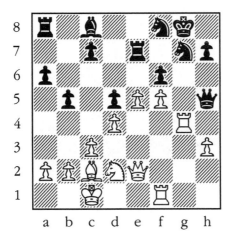

Diagram 67: White to move.

In Diagram 67, White has sacrificed a piece to reach a promising position. He has a pawn for the piece, strong pawns at e5 and f5, plus pressure down the g-file. In the long run, these factors should yield a promising attack.

But White doesn't have to wait for the long run. He can win quickly, using a discovered attack!

White plays **Rg4xg7 check!** The Rook gives check to the King, while at the same time discovering an attack on the Black Queen by the White Queen at e2. Black has no choice—he can't save his Queen because he has to deal with the check first. Black plays **Re7xg7,** and White follows with **Qe2xh5,** with a winning game.

Now let's look at some more problems using discovered attacks.

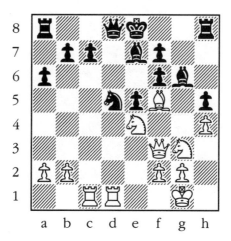

Diagram 68: White to move.

In Diagram 68, the raw material for a discovered attack is there. White's Queen on f3 has a latent attack against the Black Knight on d5. If the Knight on e4 were to move away, the Queen on f3 and the Rook on d1 would be teamed up on the d5 Knight. Making this happen in the right way, however, is a little tricky.

The direct approach is to play Ne4-c5. This uncovers the Queen's attack on the Knight. Unfortunately, it's a slow approach, and *slow approaches give your opponent time to organize a defense.* In this case, Black would play Be7xc5, and after White recaptured, Rc1xc5, Black would play c7-c6, and the Knight would be well defended.

A better approach is with the forcing move, Ne4xf6 check. Black has to respond to the check, leaving the Knight unguarded. Black would play Be7xf6 (he can't capture with the Knight, since the Knight is pinned to the Queen by the Rook on d1), and White would reply Rd1xd5. White would have won a pawn with this order of moves.

But White has an even better sequence, one which wins the game outright. The trick is to *substitute one Black piece for another*. White starts off with **Rd1xd5!** This forces Black to reply **Qd8xd5.** Now the unguarded Queen has been substituted for the guarded Knight. Finally White plays **Ne4xf6 check!** uncovering the White Queen's attack on the Black Queen. Black plays **Be7xf6,** and White wins with **Qf3xd5.**

When combinations look possible but don't quite seem to work, examine the effects of all captures. You may be able to find a substitution, as here, which makes everything fall into place.

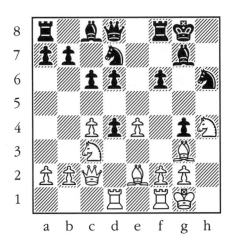

Diagram 69: White to move.

Black has just captured White's pawn on the d4 square. White could move his Knight away, but what could be more natural than simply recapturing with the Rook? However, Black has a deep trap in store, based on a discovered attack.

White, overlooking Black's plan, plays **Rd1xd4?**

Black reveals his first point; he plays **f6-f5!**

The pawn uncovers an attack by the Black Bishop on g7 against the White Rook. White, however, thinks he has plenty of time to get away. He retreats his Rook, **Rd4-d1,** evading the Bishop.

Black now reveals the real point of his combination. He pushes the pawn again, **f5-f4!** The pawn attacks the White Bishop. The Bishop has only one safe square, so White retreats again, **Bg3-h2.**

Finally Black plays **Qd8xh4!,** capturing the White Knight and emerging a piece ahead. The move of the pawn from f6 to f5 actually discovered *two* attacks, one by the Bishop on the Rook, one by the Queen on the White Knight. The latter threat didn't seem important until Black was able to chase away the Bishop defending the Knight.

Study this example carefully. In many fine combinations, the real point of attack is not visible until the very end.

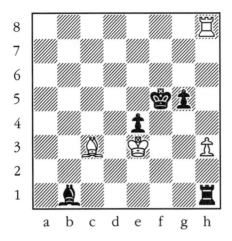

Diagram 70: White to move.

Diagram 70 is a simple-looking position. White is a pawn behind, but in no real danger of losing since Black's two remaining pawns are securely blockaded. Still, how can White be thinking of winning? And surely, there's no discovered attack in this position! Or is there?

In fact, White has an ingenious winning line, based on a discovered attack, which Black has completely over-looked. Do you see it?

White starts with a quiet little move, **Rh8-h6!!** What's this all about? Well, notice that the White Rook has cut off all the Black King's escape squares. In the starting position, the King had two squares to move to; e6 and g6. Suddenly those are both gone. What's more, White is actually threatening Rh6-f6 checkmate!

What can Black do? The Black King can't move; every open square around the King is under attack. The Black Bishop is helpless. The Black Rook can't check at e1 because the White Bishop covers that square.

The only possible move for Black is the pawn move **g5-g4,** opening an escape square for the Black King at g5. But then White pounces with **h3xg4 check,** simultaneously uncovering an attack by the White Rook on the Black one. In this case, the overpowering checkmate threat forced Black to open up the discovered attack himself!

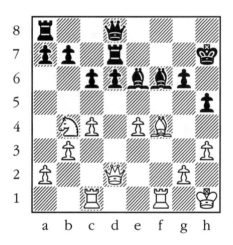

Diagram 71: Black to move.

White doesn't have a discovered attack yet in Diagram 71, but Black makes a blunder which opens up the possibility.

Black plays **Qd8-a5?,** trying to activate his Queen. White has a quick refutation planned. He moves **Nb4-**

d5!, uncovering an attack by his Queen. If Black captures, Qa5xd2, he ends up losing a piece: White would play Nd5xf6 check, and after Kh7-g7, White would play Bf4xd2, recapturing the Queen and guarding his Knight with the Rook on f1.

After Nb4-d5, Black's only chance is to retreat, **Qa5-d8.** White then plays **Nd5xf6 check,** and Black recaptures, **Qd8xf6.** Now White has a final discovered attack ready. He plays **Bf4xd6,** uncovering the attack of his Rook on Black's Queen. After Black retreats the Queen, White will protect his Bishop with **c4-c5,** remaining a solid pawn ahead.

10

DOUBLE ATTACKS

*The **double attack** (or **fork**, as it is sometimes called) is a simple but deadly tactic. You attack two of your opponent's pieces at the same time. He can protect one or the*

other, but not both. You pick off the piece he chooses not to defend. Here's a very simple example:

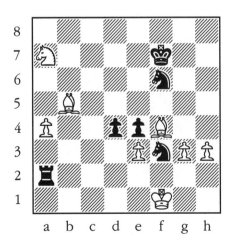

Diagram 72: White to move.

GAME EXAMPLES OF THE DOUBLE ATTACK

In a balanced but complicated game, Black has tried to make progress in the center by advancing his d-pawn from d5 to d4. He's expecting White to capture e3xd4, after which he will recapture with his Knight on f3.

But White has other plans. He ignores the pawn on d4, and instead takes note of the diagonal a2 to g8, which has been cleared by Black's last move. With Black's King and undefended Rook on the diagonal, White sees an opportunity for a devastating double attack. He plays **Bb5-c4 check!**

Black is stuck. He must save his King, which is easy enough to do, but then White picks off the Rook with **Bc4xa2**. The double attack led to an overwhelming advantage in material.

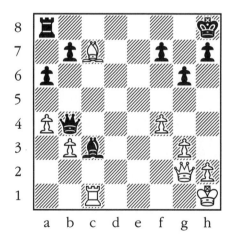

Diagram 73: White to move.

Diagram 73 is a little more complex. White notes that the diagonal a1 to h8, leading to Black's King, is wide open. White's Bishop at c7 is in position to occupy the diagonal, but to what end? If White plays Bc7-e5 check, Black just replies Bc3xe5, with an even trade of Bishops.

White needs another approach.

The trick is to force a *substitution* of one Black piece for another. With that in mind, White starts his combination with **Rc1xc3!**

By sacrificing his Rook, White forces the Black Queen to take up a place on the vulnerable diagonal. Black naturally recaptures with **Qb4xc3.** Now White plays his winning fork: **Bc7-e5 check!**

With a Black Queen on c3 rather than a Bishop, the double attack is deadly. Black has to play **Qc3xe5,** and White replies **f4xe5.** He has won a Queen for a Rook, and has a winning endgame.

The key to a double attack is to visualize two enemy pieces on the same rank, file, or diagonal, and then find a way to attack both with one of your own pieces. Often this will require some preliminary maneuvering.

Let's look at some more examples.

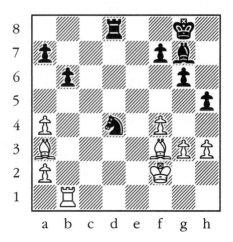

Diagram 74: Black to move

White's loose pieces scattered around the board are perfect targets for a double attack if Black can find the right approach. Again, the idea of *substituting* one piece for another holds the key.

Black starts with a capture, **Nd4xf3!** White recaptures, **Kf2xf3,** but this brings the King out toward the center of the board, where he is more vulnerable to checks. Black then exploits this vulnerability with a double attack, **Rd8-d3 check!**

The Rook attacks the White King and, simultaneously, the White Bishop over on a3. White must save his King, losing the Bishop.

ATTACKING UNATTENDED PIECES

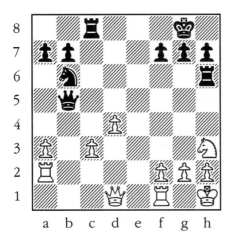

Diagram 75: Black to move.

A good exercise to develop your awareness of the board is to look around for your opponent's *undefended* pieces. Undefended pieces are ideal targets for double attacks.

In Diagram 75, the only undefended White piece is the Rook at a2. No other White piece guards that square. How can Black exploit this? He must move quickly, else White can simply play a move like Ra2-c2, with a solid, if cramped, position.

Black finds a way by examining the captures available to him. He starts a combination by playing **Rh6xh3!** White responds with **g2xh3.**

Sacrificing the Black Rook for the White Knight has opened the diagonal from c6 to h1, leading directly to White's King. With this line open, Black plays **Qb5-d5 check!**

The Queen attacks the White King along one diagonal, the White Rook along another. After the King moves, the Rook is lost, and Black will be a Knight ahead. Once again, examining the available checks and captures enabled Black to visualize the winning combination.

THE DOUBLE DOUBLE ATTACK

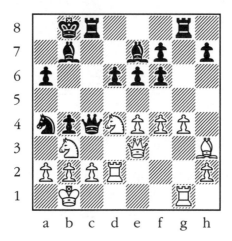

Diagram 76: Black to move.

Where's the double attack in Diagram 76? The White Queen is unguarded, but that's about it. At first glance, it's not at all clear that Black can make any progress. But by examining the possible captures and checks, Black finds a way to launch not one, but *two* double attacks!

Black starts with a sacrifice which forces White's hand. He plays **Na4xb2!**

White can't afford to let his pawn position be demolished for nothing, so he naturally recaptures, **Kb1xb2.**

Now Black springs the first double attack; he plays **Qc4-c3 check!** The Queen attacks both the White King and the undefended White Queen. Now White really has no choice. To avoid losing his Queen, he must play **Qe3xc3.**

Now the final element of the combination falls into place. Black recaptures, **b4xc3 check.** The lowly Black pawn now forks the White King and the White Rook. White has to move the King, and Black will then play **c3xd2,** emerging with a Rook for a Knight, a winning advantage.

MORE DOUBLE ATTACKS

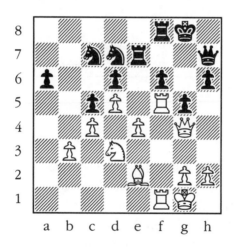

Diagram 77: White to move.

In Diagram 77 White also has the possibility of a double attack with a pawn, but it's very well-concealed. Which White pawn could possibly do Black any damage?

Watch how White breaks through the Black position. White starts with **b3-b4!** Black naturally captures, **c5xb4.**

Now White pushes the next pawn in the chain, **c4-c5!** Again, Black captures with **Nd7xc5.**

White exchanges Knights, **Nd3xc5,** and Black recaptures again with **d6xc5.**

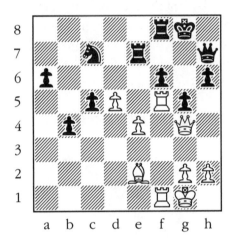

Diagram 77a

Take a look. The White pawns have acted like crowbars, gradually prying open the Black position. Now White can finish his combination with **d5-d6!** forking the Black Rook and the Black Knight. Black will save his Rook, and after capturing the Knight, White should win the endgame.

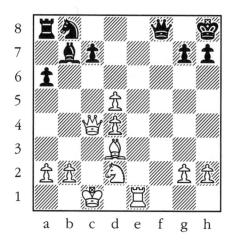

Diagram 78: White to move.

In Diagram 78, White looks around for undefended Black pieces. The Black Bishop on b7 is undefended, he notes. So is the Black Queen on f8. Is there a way to attack both those pieces simultaneously?

Well, he could play Qc4-b4. That attacks the Black Queen along the diagonal, and the Black Bishop along the file. But of course, Black would simply take the White Queen with his queen if White made that play. Or would he?

A good rule of thumb: *Double-check all potentially winning ideas.* Sometimes a play that looks absurd at first glance actually has a real point. After due consideration, White in fact plays **Qc4-b4!!**

Now Black sees to his horror that taking the White Queen leads to a quick checkmate. After Qf8xb4, White swoops down with Re1-e8 check, and after Black interposes with Qb4-f8, White delivers checkmate by Re8xf8.

With both his Queen and Bishop under attack, Black needs to find a move that saves both. He has one try, **Qf8-c8,** moving the Queen to protect the Bishop. But now White finishes him off with **Qb4xb7!** and Black discovers that he can't recapture without being checkmated as before. With an extra piece and two extra pawns, it's an easy win for White.

11

REMOVING THE GUARD

Here's the idea. Your opponent is defending one piece with another. You capture the defending piece, knocking the props out from

under the other. When your opponent recaptures, you are free to capture the other, now unguarded piece.

Here's an example:

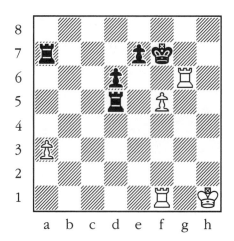

Diagram 79: Black to move.

Each side has two rooks and two pawns. White's Rook on g6 is attacked by Black's King, but securely protected by the White pawn on f5. But the pawn is itself attacked by the Black Rook. Black reasons: "The Rook is guarded by the pawn. If I eliminate the pawn, the Rook will be unguarded." Black puts his finger on the weakness in White's position and plays **Rd5xf5!**

By capturing the pawn, Black has eliminated the defense of the Rook on g6. White recaptures with **Rf1xf5** check, and Black picks off the now-undefended Rook with **Kf7xg6.** He has won a pawn and now has good winning chances in the endgame. This concept is simple when you know what to look for.

Here's another example:

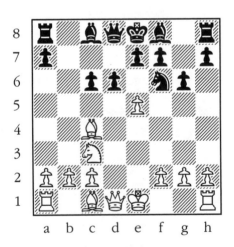

Diagram 80

White has just played e4-e5, attacking the Black Knight. Black could move the Knight (and that would be the better course) but he sees that the pawn on e5 is un-guarded. Why not just capture it? Black plays **d6xe5,** unaware that he is falling into a deep trap.

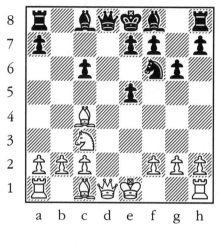

Diagram 80a

This is the position White had foreseen when he played e4-e5.

Notice that the White Queen now attacks the Black Queen. The Black Queen is adequately defended by the Black King. But suppose the Black King weren't around anymore? Then the Queen would be unguarded. Can White make this happen? Indeed he can! He plays **Bc4xf7 check!**

The Bishop sacrifices itself for the Black pawn, but lures the Black King away from its Queen. Black plays **Ke8xf7,** and White swoops down with **Qd1xd8,** remaining a Queen ahead with an easy win.

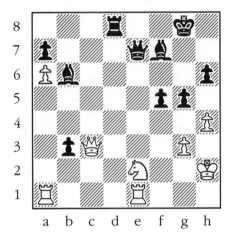

Diagram 81: Black to move.

Material is approximately even in Diagram 81. White has the advantage of a Rook for a Bishop, but Black has two extra pawns as compensation. White's position is a little disjointed, however, and that presents Black with some opportunities.

To spot opportunities for removing the guard, look for situations where pieces have to guard other pieces. In Diagram 81, Black's Queen attacks the White Knight on e2. The Knight is guarded by the Rook on e1. An opportunity exists if Black can find a way to attack the Rook. And Black, in fact, has a way. He plays **Bb6-f2!**

The Bishop attacks the Rook, but if the Rook moves, Black will take the Knight with his Queen. White will have to leave the Rook where it is, and next turn Black will play **Bf2xe1.** The exchange will leave him two pawns ahead, with a winning position.

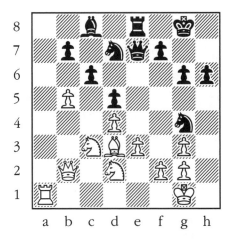

Diagram 82: Black to move.

In Diagram 82, Black's pieces are poised to make a move on the center and the King-side, but White's position, at first glance, seems secure. One possible line of attack would be Qe7-f6, attacking the pawn on f2 twice. But White could defend in a number of ways; Ra1-f1, for example, defending the pawn with the Rook, or Nd2-f3, blocking the Queen's attack. White's pieces are sufficiently well-developed and mobile so that he can rush defenders to any direct assault.

What Black needs is a lightning strike against White's position, a blitzkrieg which gives White no time to mobilize his pieces. Does such a possibility exist?

Black takes a look at White's chain of defenses. The pawn on d4 is guarded by the pawn on e3. And that pawn, in turn, is guarded by the pawn on f2, which for now, is guarded only by the King on g1. The prop of the whole

White pawn chain is the weak pawn on f2. Can Black knock out that prop?

Indeed he can. Black plays **Ng4xf2!** The Knight sacrifices itself to smash through the pawn chain before White can organize resistance. White has to reply **Kg1xf2.** Now Black swoops down with **Qe7xe3 check!** White's only move is **Kf2-f1.** Black now picks up the undefended Bishop with **Qe3xd3 check.** Next turn he will follow up with **Qd3xd4.** In return for the sacrificed Knight, Black will have netted a Bishop and three pawns–a tidy profit.

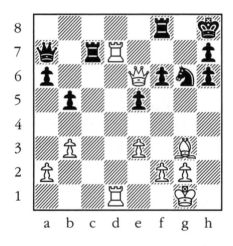

Diagram 83: White to move.

Removing-the-guard problems can be quite difficult to spot. Take Diagram 83. The key here is the Black Knight, which is guarding something vital. Just what, however, isn't obvious until we see White's inspired line of play.

White plays **Bg3-h4!!** The Bishop attacks the pawn at f6 which is impossible to defend again. But wait–isn't the

Bishop unguarded? Having little choice, Black snaps off the Bishop with **Ng6xh4.**

White gave up his Bishop to lure away the Black Knight. What was the Knight guarding that was so important? Answer–an empty square! White now plays **Qe6-e7!,** occupying a square that was previously guarded by the Knight.

Black is helpless. White is threatening Qe7xh7 checkmate, and Black can only delay the inevitable. He plays **Rc7xd7,** and White replies with **Rd1xd7.** Black gives up.

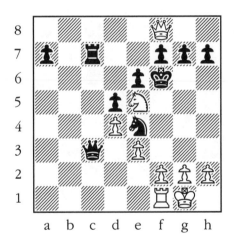

Diagram 84: White to move.

In Diagram 84, the opportunity for a removing-the-guard play exists, but White must first create the guarded piece. This he does by playing **Qf8-d8 check!**

Black has only two ways to get out of check. One way is to move the King, but that leads to a quick checkmate. If Black plays Kf6-f5, White would respond with g2-g4 checkmate!

So Black tries the other way. Interposing the Rook, he plays **Rc7-e7.**

But now White springs his trap. The Rook is guarded only by the Black King, an unstable situation as we have seen. White exploits this by playing **Ne5-d7 check!** The Knight checks the guarding King and forces it to move. Next turn White plays **Qd8xe7,** pocketing a whole Rook.

Diagram 85: Black to move.

Good defensive play in chess requires alertness. Don't assume your position is hopeless because your opponent has played a move you didn't expect. Defensive resources are sometimes available–if you look for them!

In Diagram 85, Black sees a chance to win a pawn since White's pawn at e4 is attacked twice, by the Bishop at g6 and the Knight at f6, while it's defended only by the White Knight at c3. Thinking to win a pawn easily, Black plays **Bg6xe4**.

White, however, pulls a surprise. Instead of recapturing the Bishop, which would eventually leave White a pawn down, he sees a chance for a play based on removing the guard. He plays instead **g4-g5**.

The pawn attacks the Black Knight, but if the Knight moves away, it will no longer defend the Bishop. White will then play Nc3xe4, winning a piece. If the Knight doesn't move away, of course, White expects to just play g5xf6, winning a piece in a different way.

Many players in Black's position would lose heart, conclude they'd been outplayed, and surrender the piece. Black decides to fight back! Examining his possibilities, he finds a saving shot: **Be4-c2!**

By attacking the White Queen, Black buys time. White has to move his Queen, enabling Black to save his attacked Knight next turn with **Nf6-d5**. Watch for this kind of tempo-gaining move (Be4-c2), which can be the key to saving a threatened position.

12

THE OVERWORKED PIECE

In chess, if one of your pieces has too many functions to perform, we refer to it as **overworked**. Spotting an overworked piece and exploiting its weakness is the key to many original tactics ideas.

> ### FIRST WORD
> Once you identify an overworked piece, you have a target that is vulnerable to the sharp attacking principles we'll look at in this chapter.

Take a look at Diagram 86:

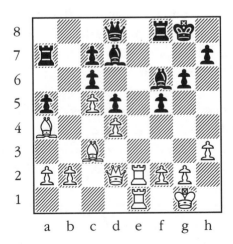

Diagram 86: White to move.

Material is even in Diagram 86, but White sees the opportunity to win a pawn. Black's pawn on a5 is guarded only by the Black Rook, while White attacks the pawn with the Bishop on c3 backed up by the Queen on d2. More attackers than defenders generally means the pawn can be taken with impunity, so White plays **Bc3xa5**. He sees that if Black tries Ra7xa5, White can reply with Qd2xa5.

Black isn't worried, however. He's seen farther into the position than White, and he's noticed a crucial point: After White captures the pawn, his Queen at d2 has become an *overworked piece*. The Queen now has two jobs. It must protect the Bishop at a5, attacked by the Black Rook, and it must also protect the pawn at d4, attacked by the Black Bishop at f6.

One piece defending two other pieces, both under attack, is an unstable situation. Black exploits the situation by playing **Bf6xd4!**

What's White to do? If he captures Black's Bishop, he will lose his own Bishop to the Black Rook. But otherwise, Black has simply won back the pawn, with a slightly better position to boot.

In Diagram 86, the overworked piece was the key to a successful defensive maneuver. Black actually saw that his pawn on a5 was *indirectly guarded* by the possibility of the combination that followed.

Now let's look at some more examples, in which the overworked piece idea is the key to some spectacular offensive combinations.

CREATING THE OVERWORKED PIECE

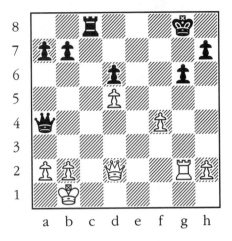

Diagram 87: Black to move.

In Diagram 87, White has no overworked piece, as yet. Black's attacking possibility seems to be directed at the squares c1, c2, and d1, and White has all those squares adequately guarded. Black will first have to create the possibility for a combination.

Black starts with a powerful check: **Qa4-e4 check!** The Queen checks the King and also attacks the White Rook at g2. At first, this doesn't look all that threatening. The Rook is guarded by the White Queen, and the White King has an escape square. White plays **Kb1-a1.** Now take a look at the new position:

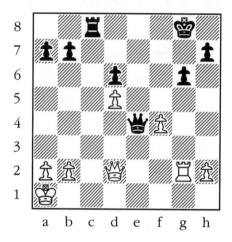

Diagram 87a

White's position holds together, but just barely. The threat of Rc8-c1 check is prevented by the White Queen at d2. The threat of Qe4-e1 check is also stopped by the White Queen. And the threat of Qe4xg2 is prevented by— yes, the White Queen again!

Clearly, the White Queen is overcommitted. It must stay exactly where it is to guard all Black's threats. Can Black find the key that exposes the fragile nature of White's position? Yes! He plays **Qe4xg2!**

White is doomed. The Queen had to guard both the Rook at g2 and the mate at c1. It couldn't do both. If White recaptures the Black Queen, Black swoops down with Rc8-c1 checkmate. Otherwise, White is a Rook down.

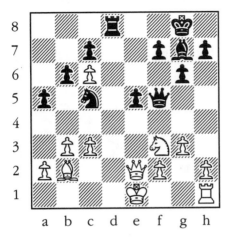

Diagram 88: Black to move.

As in the previous problem, the overworked piece does not yet exist in Diagram 88. Black must create the overworked piece. This he does with the alert play **Nc5-d3 check!** White's King must move out of check, but he wants to stay away from the d-file, since moving there would open up the possibility of a discovered check from the Rook at d8. So White plays **Ke1-f1.**

Now we see the elements of the overworked piece in place. The Black Knight at d3 attacks the White Bishop at b2. The Black Queen attacks the White Knight at f3. Both the White Bishop and the White Knight are defended by the Queen at e2.

The Queen is overworked. It can't defend both pieces at once. Black takes advantage of the situation by playing **Nd3xb2!** If White recaptures, he loses the Knight at f3.

Otherwise, he is down a Bishop. Once again, the over-worked piece can't handle its defensive assignments.

CAPTURING IN THE RIGHT ORDER

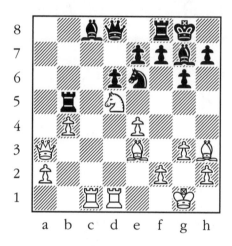

Diagram 89: White to move.

The overworked piece in this position is the Black Queen at d8. It has to guard the pawn at e7 (attacked by the White Knight) and the Bishop at c8 (attacked by the Rook at c1).

White has to be accurate, though. It won't do to begin with Nd5xe7 check, since when Black replies Qd8xe7, his Rook at f8 takes over the job of guarding the Bishop at c8.

The right way is to begin with **Rc1xc8!** Now when Black recaptures **Qd8xc8**, White has the devastating Knight fork **Nd5xe7 check!**, winning the Black Queen.

In overworked piece combinations, the order of capture

is usually crucial. Check all possibilities to make sure you find the most favorable one.

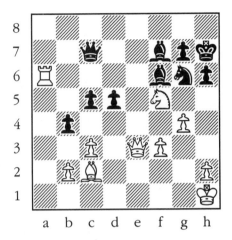

Diagram 90: White to move.

Take a look at Diagram 90 carefully. Can you spot Black's overworked piece here? It's quite well concealed.

Actually, it's the Black pawn on g7. It has a dual role–to guard the Bishop on f6, and the pawn on h6, both of which are under attack. Capturing the pawn first isn't the right way (check this out for yourself). The best approach is for White to play **Ra6xf6!** When Black recaptures **g7xf6**, the Black pawn on h6 is left undefended. White finishes the game off with **Qe3xh6 check**, Black plays **Kh7-g8**, and then **Qh6-g7** is checkmate!

13

NO RETREAT

In chess, mobility, having lots of squares to move your pieces to, is a good thing. The player with lots of mobility probably has the better position, while the player with limited mobility probably has the worse position.

FIRST WORD

In extreme cases, pieces can run out of places to move altogether. When this happens, winning is a simple matter–just attack the piece that can't move away. That's the basic idea behind the tactic called **"no retreat."**

EXPLOITING THE LACK OF MOBILITY

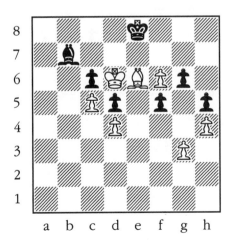

Diagram 91: White to move.

White and Black have the same material in Diagram 91, but look at the difference in mobility! White has pushed Black almost off the board. Black's King is confined to the back rank, while his Bishop hardly has any moves at all. Still, Black has managed to keep everything defended. How can White break through?

White wins by exploiting the lack of mobility of Black's Bishop, which has to defend the pawn on c6. Using his King as an offensive piece, White attacks the Bishop: **Kd6-c7!**

Black doesn't have much choice. If he loses the pawn on c6, he will then lose the pawn on d5, after which White's pawns will march up the board to Queen. The Bishop has to defend the pawn, and it can only do so from one last square: Black moves **Bb7-a8.**

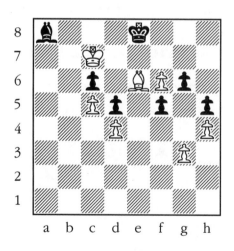

Diagram 91a

Although Black has held onto the pawn, his Bishop now

has nowhere at all to go–the ultimate condition of "no retreat." Winning the hapless Bishop is now simple: White just picks it off with **Kc7-b8!** and the Bishop is trapped.

Of course, it's unusual for one side to be as squeezed as Black was in Diagram 91. Let's look at some more examples of no retreat from earlier parts of the game.

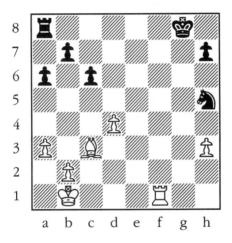

Diagram 92: White to move.

"Knight on the rim spells trim," is an old chess maxim warning of the dangers of leaving a Knight on the side of the board. As we mentioned earlier, Knights don't have much mobility on the edge of the board; try to keep your them actively placed in the center if you can.

In Diagram 92, Black has allowed his Knight to wander off to the h5 square. It doesn't appear to be in any danger, for now. Watch how quickly White changes the picture!

White starts with the surprising move **d4-d5!**, voluntarily sacrificing a pawn. (The idea is to activate the Bishop at c3.) Not seeing the danger, Black responds with **c6xd5.**

Now White springs his trap; he plays **Rf1-f5!** Black's Knight, caught on the edge of the board, suddenly has a shortage of squares to move to. The squares f4 and f6 are out of the question. If he plays Nh5-g3, White wins the Knight with the double attack Rf5-g5 check! In desperation, Black plays **Nh5-g7.** Then White finishes him off with **Rf5-g5**, winning the Knight with a pin.

On the edge square h5, the Knight only had four possible escape squares, instead of the usual eight. This lack of mobility was decisive when confronted with White's alert play.

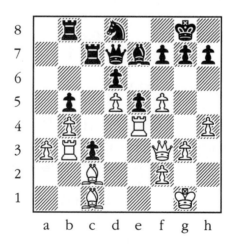

Diagram 93: White to move.

White has a strong position in Diagram 93 and elects to push ahead with a King-side attack. He plays **g3-g4!** The idea is to continue with g4-g5. The move also sets a subtle trap.

Black notices that the pawn on h4 is now unprotected. Thinking that he can now win a pawn, he plays **Be7xh4?** overlooking White's reply.

White moves **g4-g5!** anyway, and now Black sees the point. His Bishop on h4 is trapped, while the pawn move has uncovered an attack on the Bishop by the Rook on e4 (discovered attack). Black is helpless. The best he can do is to sacrifice the Bishop for the pawn on g5: **Bh4xg5.** White replies **Bc1xg5**, winning a piece.

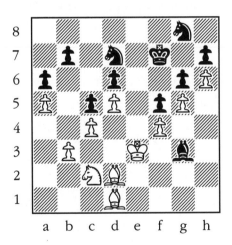

Diagram 94: White to move.

Black's Bishop has maneuvered itself into an awkward situation. At g3, it has very few squares left. Sensing the opportunity for a "no retreat" combination, White moves in for the kill: **Ke3-f3!**

Black doesn't have much choice. The square e1 is guarded by the White Bishop, while if Black tries Bg3-h2, White traps it immediately with Kf3-g2! Instead, Black tries **Bg3-h4.**

At first, it looks like the Bishop might have found a safe hiding place. If White moves his King to g2 and h3, the Bishop will slip out by moving to f2, then over to d4 and back home.

White notices that with his King guarding g3 and f2, and his Bishop guarding e1, the Black Bishop now can't move at all. White just needs a piece to actually attack the Bishop. The Knight is the logical candidate. Is there a route for the Knight to get to the Black Bishop? Yes indeed!

White plays **Nc2-e3!** His next move will be **Ne3-g2**, and then **Ng2xh4.** Black has no retreat and no defense. The Bishop is lost.

TRAPPING THE QUEEN

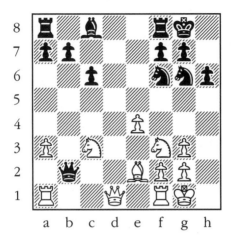

Diagram 95: White to move.

So far we've looked at examples of trapping slow-moving Bishops and Knights. What about a really powerful piece like the Queen? Surely a Queen has the range and maneuverability to flee from these little trapping combinations?

Not always. Take a look at Diagram 95. Black has just moved his Queen down to b2, capturing a White pawn in the process. The Queen also attacks the loose White Knight, so Black figures he will cause White some defensive problems and pick up a pawn in the process.

White has some other ideas. He deftly plays **Nc3-a4!** and suddenly the Black Queen is a little embarrassed. Although it has 15 legal moves, every square it can use is guarded by a White piece! The Queen is lost.

14

MOVING ON

Armed with the knowledge you've learned here, you'll see the recurring patterns of pins, double attacks, discovered checks, and all the other powerful tactical ideas long before your opponents. You'll not only be able

GOOD JOB!
You've now completed our introduction to tactical play. If you're like most players, the ideas in this book will make a tremendous difference in your game.

to carry out these maneuvers yourself, you'll be able to anticipate and thwart your opponent when he tries them on you!

At this point you may want to brush up on your opening play, to make sure that you're able to come out of the first few moves of the game with an equal or better position. (Tactical possibilities are easier to find when your pieces have more activity from the very start.) A good book for this purpose is *Winning Chess Openings*, another book in the "Road to Chess Mastery" series. Look for it at the same bookstore where you bought this volume, or order directly from Cardoza Publishing.

Don't forget to get out and actually play some chess.

Look for a chess club in your area. (*Beginning Chess Play* has some good tips for finding your local clubs.) Look for other opponents at work or school. Challenge people to play. With the knowledge you've acquired here, you'll be successful against most of the people you meet.

Keep reading, keep playing, and keep winning!
